I0393513

Losing the Cape

Strategies to move your business from chaos to control

(c) 2017 Smartspeed Consulting Limited. All rights reserved.

Disclaimer:

The author of this book has tried to present the most accurate information to his knowledge at the time of writing. This book is intended for information purposes only. The author does not imply any results to those using this book, nor are they responsible for any results brought about by the usage of the information contained herein.

No part of this book may be reprinted, electronically transmitted or reproduced in any format without the express written permission of the author.

Introduction

Welcome to 'Losing the Cape'.

This book is written for the manager that wants to get better results from their business.

It is written for the person that feels frustrated with how their day works out and wants to experience a more fulfilling and results rich time during their employment.

For business owners this book holds a number of strategies that can ultimately help you to win more business, have fewer headaches and increase the value of your business.

In a moment I will start to share with you my views on the superhero capes that exist within businesses.

Part one will give you some ideas to think about and hopefully change your perspective on what the reactive incidents in your business really mean.

Part two will then take you through a series of practical ideas, strategies and methods to help you turn your business from a frenetic, often chaotic, place to a more orderly, productive, fun and profitable place. Whether you choose to follow all of the ideas in the book, or just the ones that feel right to you right now, the objective of the book is the same.

I want you to transform your business into a better version of itself, the version you know it can be. And, if you happen to get promoted, increase your earnings or have more fun as a result of being part of this transformation, that would be the icing on the cake.

Ok, are you ready to start looking for capes?

Giles Johnston

September 2017

Table of Contents

Part One – The Cape

Are you ready to start to hunt for the capes present in your business?

If I do my bit right, and you come along for the hunt, you should be able to see some of the past events of your business differently. Between us we can find opportunities for improvement by changing the meaning we give to certain events.

On your mark, get set, go!

What Is the Cape?

Welcome to this book. I see many people who 'love the cape' whilst on my travels as I work with businesses to improve their on time delivery and productivity levels. When there is a problem in their business these individuals, like a superhero, change from their normal personality into someone who can leap into the heart of the action and remedy the situation.

The cape is a habit pattern; when there is a problem they leap into action and achieve a better result. When there is a (perceived) emergency in the business the cape appears.

The cape is everywhere

Let me give you some examples of when the cape might appear.

Imagine you work in a factory and you are regularly behind schedule with your orders. When you get customers phoning you to complain about orders being late the cape might come out. Overtime might be arranged, extra labour might be sourced and other deliveries might be sacrificed. You manage to please the customer who has complained... but at a cost.

Now imagine that you are working on a project and the deadline is looming. You realise that in order to avoid the penalties that the customer will impose you need to 'pull out all of the stops'. Like the last example, overtime and additional labour may be applied. Hopefully corners won't be cut, but you are no longer sure as the pressure of the situation increases. The productivity of the project increases during this period… but it leaves a nasty taste in the mouth.

So, is there an alternative?

Why do we need the cape in the first place?

Why Do We Need the Cape?

The cape fascinates me. I am writing this in in 2017 and most of the problems I deal with when I work with businesses (in all different sectors) are to do with fundamentals. My father once asked me about what kind of improvement projects I work on and he was disappointed to hear that I wasn't working on some kind of high tech / state of the art problem. I was working on problems that were the same problems that he would have faced decades earlier. This is not meant to depress you, rather encourage you that you are not facing a new set of challenges, just a different environment to apply some age-old wisdom.

Are you exceptional?

Getting the basics right in most businesses can be enough to distinguish you from the competition. Being exceptional often means doing the basics extraordinarily well.

The cape exists when an unforeseen issue hits the business. It exists because we need some immediate results and we need a superhero level response to get the business unstuck, fast!

When I say unforeseen this is not entirely true. There are some genuine issues that need to be dealt with that not even the best strategist could foresee. But, and this is the point of this book, there are a whole range of other issues that could have been foreseen. They haven't come out of the blue, they have been lurking amongst the weaknesses of the business. They shouldn't be a surprise, but they do catch us off-guard.

A lack of systems?

Many of the times the cape needs to appear is because we have failed to create the type of systems and processes in our business that help us to stop these issues from arising in the first place. I am not going to give you a false picture of the world. Sometimes stuff just happens, what I am going to suggest in this book is that we are the creators of a lot of this stuff. The illustration below will hopefully ring a bell with you.

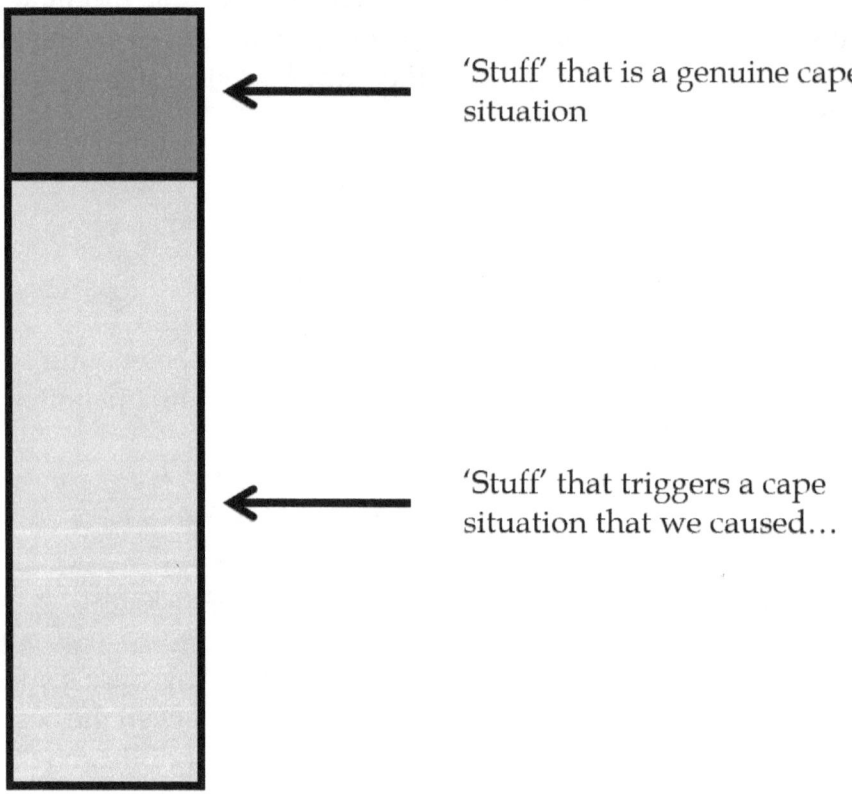

'Stuff' that is a genuine cape situation

'Stuff' that triggers a cape situation that we caused...

As I write this I am thinking back to a time when I used to run a business unit within a manufacturing plant. Every day was a challenge to juggle the despatches planned for the day just to minimise the level of complaints that I received. My cape didn't get me the kind of recognition that would be portrayed in a film, it just reduced the 'beating' I would receive from the people who paid our bills. The bottom line was that I was trying to wear the cape continuously, not achieving the results needed and getting progressively more tired. Our customers were unimpressed and my business unit was making a loss.

It was only when I got fed up with this situation that I put the cape away for only genuine crisis situations. I had to think differently; I could no longer think like the people who were around me who were in the same basic position as me. If I wanted different results I had to do something different.
So, that is why the cape exists, to cater for both genuine emergencies and our own inadequacies in terms of running a business.

When I left the cape for only very occasional use my business unit soared. The team work increased, the profits returned (and were improved upon each month for the rest of my time there), new products were introduced faster and our overall productivity was on an upwards trajectory. I actually spent less time in the factory and enjoyed the job more.

I'm not going to guarantee any results from this book, but I hope that you can find a number of strategies that you can use to form more productive habits in your business that can make your life a little easier and help your business to perform at a higher level.

'Out of the Blue Cape' Versus 'Repeat Cape'

Let me make a clarification at this point about the two types of cape I see on regular basis. I really need to stress this point before I carry on.

The genuine cape

When you have a genuine crisis in your business you need to put on the cape and do what is necessary. In these instances, you are caught off guard and have to do something in order to avert disaster. Disaster obviously differs depending on your particular industry and your business' perception of what bad looks like, but you will know what disaster looks like for you.

These crises are often things that have such a low probability of happening that they aren't part of your business forecast. They don't make up part of your plans and therefore leave you unprepared for their occurrence. They appear to be out of the blue.

The fake cape

The other type of cape situation is the type that you can predict, the type that you have seen before and pretty much guarantee that you'll see again. These repeat incidents require for the cape to be worn because you need to sort out the situation. You might even realise that you have caused the issue that raised the crisis in the first place; there might have been something that you haven't been doing that has led to this situation.

Both of these situations require the cape to be worn and it is likely that you will never get away from the need to have a cape in your business, to some degree. So, here's the challenge. Can you do something about the repeat crises that lowers the overall need to do your superhero act on such a regular basis?

I want to add at this point that if your business is facing a resource issue, if your staff are stretched beyond what is realistic then some of the cape situations you are experiencing are likely to be exacerbated by this factor. There is some good news to be found in this book however. Before you look at your resource plan and start to plan out what level of staff you need to operate your business, read this book first. Once you have worked your way through the different ideas and options you should be in a better position to design how you want your business to operate. You may even find that you are able to stop doing some of the things you are doing currently, and this might free up some of the time that has been tied up wearing unnecessary capes. Additionally, if resource management is a missing process in your business then after you have reviewed the ideas in this book you may decide to include it as a formal activity going forward.

If you split up the crises your business faces into two camps; out of the blue and repeat crises you would have a ratio you could monitor. Over time, following the ideas in this book, you should be able to see a significant decrease in the repeat cape incidents and even possibly a reduction in the out of the blue incidents.

You will still have urgent issues to deal with, but the ones caused within your business will decrease if you actively work on the causes that are under your control.

Action Points

- Make a distinction between the genuine capes and the unnecessary capes that appear in your business.

Do Crises Hide a Skills Shortage?

A question that must come to mind is 'do crises hide skills shortages within my business?'

It is a perfectly valid question and one this book is built on.
In my experience it is hard to see what shortcomings people's skill sets have when they spend their time in superhero mode.

Whilst preparing to write this book I asked a number of business owners and directors their opinion to this question and got the same answer. Over time it was felt that if they didn't move away from the fire fighting and chaos mode then it was assumed that the person in question didn't have the skills / habits to work in a different way.

One person in particular said "they might have the skills, but they don't seem to choose to use them, they seem happy flying around putting out fires."

Interesting...

What if there is no second mode?

Appraisals and regular reviews with your staff are a good place to start to try and work out if there is anything more to an individual's skill set than what you have seen.

I'm sure that you have been through enough of these conversations to realise that you need to properly dig to find out if there is a second mode to the way a person works. Most of these kinds of conversations ("we need to do something different...") lead to head nodding and the right kinds of words being said.

Pointed examples and proper responses to the questions, rather than glib generalised statements (that possibly have been trotted out several times before) need to be requested. In the heat of the discussion it is very easy for the person being questioned to tell you what you want to hear rather than the truth of the matter.

Strategies to consider

If you are thinking that some of your staff don't have a second mode don't worry, the rest of this book is here to help with that.

Of course, if you have some genuine skill deficits then it is probably worthwhile addressing those needs. However, and this is the main point of this book, the habits, processes and working patterns that we utilise in our business is what drives the main chunk of results we get.

Through the course of this book I will share with you a number of strategies that will help you to re-direct your staff in order to work in a way that is more organised and productive.

If you have read Stephen Covey's brilliant book 'The 7 Habits of Highly Effective People' you will possibly recall his views on time management and the challenge we all have - to balance our work between the important items and the urgent items. The cape lives in the world of urgency, whilst routines and process thinking live in the world of the important.

Keep reading and let's consider a simple principle that can help us to start moving in the right direction.

Action Points

- Look at the recent crises that have happened in your business. Do your team members have the right skills to avoid these crises in the future? If not, identify what skills are missing and address them.

Process Thinking Versus 'Bits' Thinking

I want to draw a distinction at this point. There is a big difference between process thinking and what I call 'bits' thinking. Being clear about this difference for your own business can help you to make a jump in the level of performance your business can make and will prepare your mind nicely for the following sections.

What are the bits?

The bits I am referring to are the individual orders, tasks and project actions that make up the work content of your business' day-to-day activities. Bits are any type of work that make up the volume of someone's day. Whether you recognise the bits of your working day, or not, is not essential at this moment in time.

Identifying your processes

Behind the bits of your day-to-day activities are your business processes. As I write this I am hoping that you are fully aware of your business' processes, whether formal or informal. I am still surprised by the amount of people I come across during my consulting travels that tell me that their business can't work using processes because everything they do is different. However, when I look at these businesses, and step back from their day-to-day activities, there is always a generic process sitting behind the frenzied activity.

If you only follow the bits...

So, the point of this quick pit-stop is to help you wake your team up to the problem of only working in the world of bits. If you focus solely on the bits of your business' production / service activities then you run the risk of not managing the wider performance of the business. People who are focussing only on the bits within the business are expert cape wearers in many cases, although many of these types of cape wearers are spotted still trapped inside the burning building!

Bits get you thinking short term and this can push the 'not critical yet' tasks into a less visible portion of the working day. Probability suggests that once these process orientated tasks become less visible they won't get executed. When you don't manage the process tasks this will lead to you to get more involved with day-to-day 'production' and ultimately micro-managing orders (the bits) through your business. Capes on standby everyone...

Moving into processes

Pure process management isn't what I'm selling here, but moving into process management is. There will still be times when you, as a manager, need to keep a special eye on the bits moving through your business. There will be project actions that will be critical that you will need to follow keenly. There will be manufacturing orders that will need a little extra attention. There will be customers that will occasionally need an extra dollop of support whilst they 'onboard', and so on.

How you move from purely bits management to process management with selective bits management is one of the questions this book will answer as you progress through its chapters. For now I want you to be aware of the bits, processes and capes that live in your business.

What if you only work on bits?

Before I move on to look at the world of 'cause and effect' you might be wondering what needs to happen next if you only work on bits. I suggest that you take a time out to look at how the bits flow through your business. Look for the commonality of what happens and you will soon spot the overall process. Identify the different gates, triggers and staff / teams that process the bits. Once you have pulled this together you will have a good idea of the process you are actually immersed in.

To access a free worksheet to help you review your business processes, visit the downloads page via the Links chapter.

Ok, so everyone fits into a process whether they realise it or not, so let's move on to look at 'cause and effect' and what it does inside your business.

Action Points

- Make sure that your business processes are formally identified and listed out.
- Look for the instances in your business where you manage by 'bits' rather than processes.

Cause and Effect Thinking

At the heart of what I have been discussing so far is the principle of 'cause and effect'.

I'm sure that this principle is not new to you. How we apply this to our thinking and our businesses however is something that is rarely consistent.

Do you live at cause?

What a question! Do you?

When you live at cause you increase the level of control you have.

When you live at effect problems are amplified, results are sometimes confusing and, frankly, it can lead to days that finish before they really start.

People who operate from a more causal perspective often appear more organised, calmer and generally get better results for the amount of effort they expend.

Change your focus to get different results

There have been a number of items we have touched upon already that come from the cause end of the spectrum; habits, processes and routines.

If you start to think about these three things, and start to make a conscious effort to move your daily activities toward them, results can change.

I can recall many businesses that I have worked in, both as an employee and as a consultant, where the chaotic working was directly related to working at the wrong end of the cause and effect continuum, as shown below.

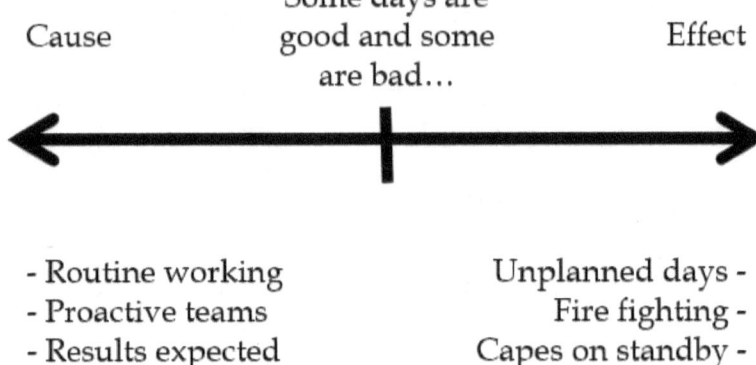

Cause   Some days are good and some are bad…   Effect

- Routine working   Unplanned days -
- Proactive teams   Fire fighting -
- Results expected   Capes on standby -

A Transport Manager used to spend every weekend planning the forthcoming deliveries whilst everyone else was at home. Two minor changes to the way he managed his days and weekend working was a rarity as the planning was completed before he left each Friday.

A Production Team Leader pulled his hair out each day as he only just managed to meet customer demands despite all of the hard work he, and his team, put into the business. By changing the questions he asked at the start of his shift, he improved the flow of product into his area and made his working life so much easier.

A Designer realised that the confusion, lateness and frustration experienced in the business were linked to not doing a few basic things each day and each week. Once identified, and the habits formed, the confusion disappeared, the work was completed on time and the frustrations lessened.

These aren't made up examples, these are a tiny fraction of the experiences my clients have had when moving their thinking from effect to cause. Living at cause doesn't eliminate all problems, but it does make life more manageable. When it's manageable, performance can shine through.

Lots of little things add up

The knock-on effect of primarily spending our time 'at cause' is that the bigger 'at effect' crises arise less frequently. There really is a snowball effect when you fail to undertake the right actions at the right time.

A decision that isn't taken today gets wrapped up with another problem brewing in the business. If the appropriate business checks aren't then completed then the slightly bigger problem starts to back up with a whole load of other issues with one of your customers and then, one day, seemingly out of the blue a crisis hits the business. The customer is going mad, it feels as though the whole business is falling apart and you need someone to jump in with their cape. The situation is resolved. The customer doesn't feel too aggrieved and we go back to normal... waiting for the next situation to arise (as we repeat the cycle).

Little things really can stack up when we don't tackle them in an appropriate manner. This is good news for us; losing the cape might just be a series of small changes to the way that we conduct both ourselves and our work.

So, where do we start with all of this?

Action Points

- Look back at how your business operates and decide whether its operates mainly from a position of cause, or effect.
- Do the same review, but this time considering how you operate. Are you mainly a cool calm operator at cause, or stuck in effect mode?
- Identify any obvious changes / improvements you would like to make to change this balance.

What Does 'Good' Look Like to You?

Many businesses that have repeated problems cropping up in their day to day work often have people working in them that don't know what 'good' looks like.

This might seem to be a strange thing to say. Surely people do know what a good way of operating a business looks like, you might be asking yourself. If I hadn't had lots of conversations about this over the years I would have agreed with you... let me give you some examples.

One business owner was telling me that their sales were dropping off. After asking a few questions it turned out that the level of activity required by the sales team (measured in this case as the number of meetings per week) was far different to the level that was required, based on their current conversion rate. The sales team didn't appear to know what good looked like.

A factory manager was grumbling because his scheduling staff spent all of their time expediting orders. When we sat down as a group it was clear that (despite having clear job descriptions) the actions that were expected from the role were not being carried out. They didn't know what a successful day looked like and hadn't twigged that by doing a few other tasks they could largely eliminate the frantic running around that they spent their days doing.

A project manager was causing a headache for the business' directors due to the crush and conquer approach to management that was being used, rather than ensuring that the project's stage gates were being achieved. The project manager had one mode of working and it wasn't a good fit for what the business was trying to achieve. This person didn't recognise that good did not look like a beaten up supply chain and demotivated staff, whilst still managing to miss all of the critical deadlines.

Can you see people in your business that don't know what good looks like and that are stuck in a rut?

Does wearing the cape look good?

This is the obvious question. If you have some idea of what you want your business activities to look like, how good is your current way of working?

When you describe someone as wearing a cape the first time they are likely to get defensive. Understandable. But, when you start to look at what has to take place in order for the business to function as normal, an interesting picture is often painted.

For most businesses the cape does not look good, it looks inefficient, difficult and it seems odd that in this day and age we cannot work in a better way.

To help you move from cape dependency to a process driven and organised way of working you will need to contrast what is happening today with what good looks like.

Defining the vision of what looks good

Logically the way out of this situation is to define what good looks like for your business. As with any kind of visioning exercise there are no fast and hard rules as to how you need to do this.

Here are a few considerations, however, to help you get started:
- Who do you want to be involved with the visioning exercise?
- Do you want to do it as a whole business, or as a smaller group / department first and then share the vision for comment / input?
- Are there any areas of the business that need to be prioritised?
- Are there any areas of the business that you would want to exclude from the exercise at this time?
- Are there any current strategic issues that you would need to weave into your vision?

If this sounds daunting to you, let's consider a relatively easy way to define our vision for the business in terms of what good looks like.

One chunk of the vision at a time?

Like many other kinds of continuous improvement activities, biting off more than you can chew is a recipe for procrastination and delay. Creating a vision may seem a little nebulous in terms of how you go about this. In my experience the quality of visions for a business are often dependent upon the person visioning and their ability to articulate what they see. Whilst the method I am about to share with you isn't fool proof you should be able to use it to make the process of generating a meaningful vision easier.

Here it is.

1. Split your business up into as many departments / functions / processes as makes sense for how you work. Don't worry about overlaps.
2. For each element that you have defined agree on what its purpose is.
3. Consider 'cause and effect' and determine what kinds of actions need to take place in order for that element to live up to its purpose whilst avoiding any crises that you have experienced in that area.
4. Work out who needs to do what, when and where in order for these actions to become a reality.
5. Write up the vision for this element as a series of bullet points, for ease of review.
6. Repeat steps 2 to 5 for the remaining elements.

If the above feels a little formulaic for you, use whichever parts of it make sense to you and discard the rest!

An example of the above (taken from one of my kind clients) is as follows:

Goods Inward (GI)

- Items are booked into the computer system within 1 hour of receipt, by the Team Leader.
- The Quality Control queue is the bible for goods inward inspection.
- GI is clear every evening, with every pallet having a batch label.
- Only GI staff sign for deliveries and they are responsible for goods until booked in.
- Booking accuracy is consistently over 98%.

This very same method was used by one of my clients who had spent several months fixing a range of operational problems in their business. Momentum was starting to wain and we needed something for the team to buy in to, so that they could move from a phase of fixing problems into a phase of becoming excellent.

Conjuring a vision wasn't working well with the people allocated to the task, and so I offered the above method. Within an hour the team were looking at the first draft and it became adopted that day as the vision for becoming excellent.

To access a free worksheet to help you define your utopian vision, visit the downloads page via the Links chapter.

When you have your vision, you'll be pleased to know that you have more than just a document to store on your server.

You now have a compass

Having a map for improving how your business works is useful. Having a compass makes having a map even more effective. With the two items in tandem you can work on the improvements for your business with absolute certainty that you are on the right path. If something knocks your plans off course a compass can help you to correct and get back on track. With only a map, getting back on track is sometimes a difficult task. Your vision is the compass.

You haven't created your improvement map yet, but that is what you are going to look at as we progress through our time together. I should also mention that I believe that there are two kinds of improvement maps.

The first is the one you need when things aren't going well, when the business is broken in some shape or form. When basic processes and activities aren't going as planned and the results are limited because something is missing (or not being done) then you need a plan that will fix what needs to be fixed.

The second type of improvement map is the one that can take you from a place where most facets of the business are going reasonably well to a situation where you are in the territory of being excellent. The mindset to move from OK to excellent is different to the one that gets the business from bad to OK. In my opinion it is why so many continuous improvement programmes fall over, they settle for OK.

This book is looking to relieve you from the need to use the cape as often as your business currently appears to need it. This vision that you have created is designed to keep you on track during both phases of improvement. By the time you have finished reading this book I expect that you will have an improvement plan for fixing the things in your business that are deemed to be broken. The gaps you can identify between where you are today and where your vision takes you to should give you the blueprint for your second phase improvement plan.

This is what I mean by the term compass; any time you have a problem with your improvement activity and you need to pull your team back on track, you have a means by which to effectively re-direct their activities. Having the vision that you have created will take you past being OK. I hope that you want to move from the problems you are experiencing in your business into a state of excellence and not just 'getting by'.

Before we get into the detail of what you can do to start losing the cape in your business we need to answer the following question...

Action Points

- Decide what good looks like for your business. Specify behaviours and standards as well as the effects that you want to witness.
- Pull the items together to form your utopian view of the world.
- Communicate your utopia to your teams.

Is it Time to Lose the Cape?

You might be thinking to yourself that this seems like a really daft question to ask.

You purchased this book because you want something to change in your business, or are looking for some approaches that you can keep up your sleeve that will help you move from chaotic working into a more controlled approach.

So why the question?

Many people like wearing a cape and it can be tricky to convince them that there is a better way. I will cover strategies later on in this book to develop your business so that these people do not have to wear the cape as often, but first let's have a think about if now is the right time to lose the cape.

What are the benefits of a cape?

Some people love wearing the cape. It might be because they don't know how to operate any other way, or that they love the feeling of being the hero when it's crunch time. Whatever their reason it is quite possible that they feel good when wearing the cape and this can become their normal way of working if they wear the cape on a regular basis.

If it is because they don't know any better, it might be the benefit of feeling comfortable with what they know, rather than venturing out into the unknown.

If it is because they like being the hero, it could be the

adoration they receive when they get the company out of trouble once more.

I'm sure that there are as many reasons to wear the cape as there are people who wear them. The two points I mention above are the two most common reasons that that I see (and I must stress it is my opinion only) on my travels in and out of different businesses.

The point to consider, when thinking about the benefits that these cape wearers may be receiving, is to ask this question:

Are you ready to make your heroes feel uncomfortable with a different way of working?

How about the benefits of losing the cape?

Let me give you a few examples of what some of my clients have really gained from losing their capes.
- More time at home with their family.
- Easier and more productive working relationships with colleagues and subordinates.
- Being able to move out of fire-fighting and into delivering against strategic objectives.
- A feeling of accomplishment of having sorted out the problems.
- Promotion, from being recognised as being a person who can sort things out.
- Lower blood pressure!

If you are fortunate, you may be able to determine something better for your current cape wearers to move towards (for them personally). Although I am asking if you are ready to make your cape wearers uncomfortable by going through a process of change (away from what they are used to), you may have the opportunity to give them a carrot to entice them. You may not have to rely on the stick only!

You need to invest the time

If losing the cape was as easy as just deciding to lose it, wouldn't it be gone already?

Identifying where the cape is being worn, why it is being worn, what needs to happen to lose it, and then managing the actions to implement the change will take time.

It will take energy, perseverance and, at times, courage.

I want you to walk into this period of change with your eyes open; it will take time and potentially take you down dead ends as you experiment with new and better approaches for your business.

Are you willing to put the time and effort into losing the cape, until the cape is only brought out for 'special occasions'?

Beware of 'going feral'!

When trying to change how a business works we run the risk of people revolting and going back to a more basic set of behaviours (their original operating programme). I often talk to my clients about people 'going feral', referring to when people appear to operate on a near survival mode when they drop their usual business practices.

New approaches to learn, new behaviours to adopt and new accountabilities can have a detrimental effect on those around us.

It has always been the case that there will be some people who will embrace new ways of working, a majority who will go with the flow (over time at least) and a handful who either are stubborn or scared and so will hold onto their current position or, if you are unlucky, move in the opposite direction.

With any kind of change taking place in a business there is the risk of losing a few people along the way. I am not necessarily talking about dismissing people, or them choosing to leave the business of their own accord. I am referring to them going feral and operating in a way that is not recognised formally by the business. The cape wearers of old may choose to ignore the new protocols so that they can keep wearing the cape (for example if they don't want to engage with the new planning process and instead want to keep 'winging it' and rescuing the business as required). These situations need to be foreseen and dealt with as they arise.

Are you ready for the inevitable drop off when people don't want to comply with your new ways of working?

So, what's your decision?

Are you ready to start making some changes in your business? If I haven't put you off by mentioning all the above (I did say that I wanted you to have your eyes wide open) then let's move forward and start to create something we can use to convert our vision into a workable approach.

Action Points

- Figure out what the response will be to your crusade to lose the capes in your business.
- Walk into the improvement activities with your eyes wide open.

Part Two - Strategies

Now that you are fully conversant with what the cape is, what it looks like and where it lives, it is time for us to look at some strategies to change this situation.

The following methods of improving how your business works will do more than just help you to remove the capes that exists within it. The ideas will also help you achieve a higher level of organisation and discipline, leading to higher levels of performance.

You don't need to apply all the ideas. Even the application of a couple of the ideas can be enough to transform the way your business operates.

Enjoy reading the ideas, then try out the methods and decide what makes the most sense for you and your business.

Guiding Principles

At this point you should now have:

   i. A vision to help you move to a more productive and more effective way of working.

  ii. A commitment to go for this, and ride out any bumps you experience along the way.

 iii. The expectation that we are going to go hunting for the causes of our need to wear capes, and eliminate them!

This chapter of the book is designed to help you build some guiding principles; these are behaviours that we want to exhibit in our business that will help us move from our current way of working toward our vision.

The next step from having a vision

Having a vision is great, but if it was that easy to achieve we would be experiencing it already. Logic dictates, from our 'cause and effect' thinking, that you will need to approach your business differently if you want a different result. This is where our principles come in.

Think of the guiding principles as the style of your new approach.

The vision tells your business where you want to go to.

The principles tell your team how you need to approach this journey.

Once you have this firmly in your head (or written down, preferably!) you can move on to look at how you can spot and eliminate the unnecessary capes present in your business, leading you to creating your action plan(s) for improvement.

At that point you should be in possession of the vision, the plan and the general approach. That's where your fun really starts!

Think strategy with a small 's'

Guiding principles (for behaviour) work so well because they are usually few in number and easy to remember. If you get everyone to agree to the principles (and I very rarely meet anyone who wants to refuse them) then it becomes an easy way to get people back on track.

I call it strategy with a small 's' because these behavioural strategies supplement your main business strategies. In the case of this book the vision forms part of your business' improvement strategy.

The day-to-day execution of strategies is about getting the days to work out right, so that the resulting weeks, months and years drop into place and help you execute your main strategies. Let me give you a quick example.

One of my clients has a handful of these guiding principles, one of them being **"lead by example"**. Nothing profound I hear you say, but having it agreed (and written down) is where the power is in this example.

One of this client's main strategies for the business was to roll out some new systems for how they were working operationally (and there were a number of Health and Safety related issues wrapped up in there too). A senior member of staff was spotted not adhering to what had been agreed by the business and, when approached, they shrugged off the need to comply, citing their seniority in the business. This subject was brought up in a management meeting later that day and, as you could imagine, an argument about time, planning and effectiveness ensued.

All it took was for one person to stand up, walk to their guiding principles 'poster' and point at "lead by example" and silently wait for the conversation to cease for the necessary effect to occur. The point was made, we all laughed at the absurdity of the situation (it seemed a logical argument to this person at the start of the conversation) and we were all able to easily move on.

That's the point of having these principles. Times can get tough, we can get knocked off course, and having a simple management tool to get us back on track is vital.
It's like being in a three-legged race. We all need to move in the same direction, at the same speed at the same time. Think of the guiding principles approach to be like this.

I'll now run through some standard principles that I have found to be useful over the years.

Example principles

To help you form your own handful of guiding principles let me share with you some of the principles that have helped me, my employers and my clients over the years.

"Data flows, it never stops."
Information comes from data, and if it is inconsistent in terms of how it moves through a business, it can make decision making hard. Good data affects everything. If you are delivering an improvement project, for example, you will need constant feedback in order to make the right decisions on how to improve the results it is producing; a regular flow of data is essential. I like this principle particularly because I am a talkative soul and get frustrated when people fail to share useful information as it often effects my personal performance. It is also vital if you are using any form of business information system (such as a CRM or ERP system). Without data flowing easily you risk making poor decisions (or no decision at all) and then have to rely on the cape being brought out to save the day.

"Production is always planned and appropriate targets are set."
What production means in your business will be different to what other people refer to, and it may in fact be better worded as 'service'. The underlying issue is that planning needs to take place in the majority of situations before the execution takes place. Failure to plan is a great reason why the cape has to appear. The phrase 'fail to plan, plan to fail' hasn't stood the test of time for no reason! Having appropriate targets is important so that we can all agree on what 'good looks like' and work to the right tempo in the business, again reducing the need to rescue the business from disaster when the time comes.

"Preparation equals productivity."
Preparation ties in with the planning activity in my opinion. Having the plan is one thing, but jumping straight into the execution phase doesn't always give the best results in terms of efficiency. Dropped efficiency can put you in weak position when it comes to delivering on your business' promises and

again raises the reliance on wearing the cape to get you out of sticky situations.

As I am writing this book there is an advert on television which depicts an aircraft where the passengers are listening to the Captain of the aircraft explaining that to save time he has done some quick checks (rather than the full pre-flight checklist). As you can imagine, the passengers get into a frenzy trying to leave the craft!

A few moments / minutes / hours of preparation can give a real boost to productivity and this can often be an anti-cape strategy in its own right.

"Take pride in the workplace."

Most of the principles that make up this list are good habits. Good habits spread. If you are disciplined in one area then there is a good chance that you will be disciplined in another. Taking pride in the workplace is one of these good habits and it can rub off onto most of the people you work with. If the workplace is looked after people behave differently and to get a different result you will need different behaviours.

If the workplace looks battered and beaten up then the rules and requirements of the business will be treated differently to a business that has a well looked after feel about it. If you want any corroboration of this point have a look at how people treat their cars; the nice shiny ones are nice and shiny because they get looked after better (in general) to the beaten up ones.

If you do happen to have a beaten up looking business at the moment consider sprucing some parts of it up. People will notice it, it will have an effect on them and that leads me nicely to the next principle…

"Lead by example."

You cannot expect the people working for you in the business to behave and operate in a way that you want if you don't do something identical (or at worst, very similar). In the last two weeks (as I write this) I have been faced with two business owners who were complaining about the Health and Safety behaviours of their staff, one of which I mentioned just a moment ago. These same people flouted their own rules and then complained when others did the same thing. As you can imagine I tackled this conversation diplomatically, but they agreed that they weren't leading by example. Within days of our conversations their workforce were behaving differently because these two individuals started to be prominent with their own PPE (Personal Protective Equipment) and adhering to the safety rules of the business.

This isn't rocket science. If you follow the logic that leaders have followers and the followers are always watching – watching what the expected standards are, you can take advantage of this. This one principle alone has the power to transform the performance of a business.

"Take your work seriously, but not yourself (or others)."
It's important that we think we are good at our jobs. It's important that we make decisions with confidence. It is also important that we don't get too caught up in our own hype!

The work we are doing needs to be taken seriously and we need to respect both ourselves and our colleagues. When we get arrogant about our own performance, or worried about what people think of us, it is at the expense of the business' performance. If you absorb all of the baggage that comes along with working day to day, it can become tiresome. So, this principle is about letting some of the irritations go and not being part of that scene.

Focus on the process, focus on getting it right. Focus on having good working relationships with your colleagues and team members. Focus on the small things each day that will help you have brilliant business days.

Try to forget about the fact that your colleagues have their own human issues to deal with – talking too much, not writing things down and not delivering when they said they would. Take their personalities away from the conversations and keep it to the business processes at hand. This way you can get to shorter meetings, clearer action plans, effective to do lists and meetings that have clearer obligations and deadlines.

We're all experiencing our working days differently. Some of us love them, some of us hate them and some appear indifferent. This principle is about taking the frustration out of the weaknesses we all bring with us as human beings.

"Routines are established and maintained."

For me, one of the most important things a business can do is get clear on what their normal working days and weeks look like. Some businesses refer to this as a 'day in the life of...' or 'business as usual' and it helps to bring structure to a working environment.

Whenever a business is in chaos (and uses the cape on a very frequent basis) they often don't have a clear structure in place. I hear the arguments against this principle that go along the lines of 'every day is different here' and 'we can't plan how we work, we just have to react'. I could go on, but the basic message is the same – in effect the message is 'we are in a state of chaos and think that planning our time and activities is pointless'.

As you would hope, once I hear this kind of comment (it's a little like a red rag to a bull!) we often find the basic, generic, tasks that can drive a different level of performance. These tasks usually have a logical point in the day, or week, when they need to be triggered. And, hey presto, the weeks take form and structure appears.

It is most likely that because you are reading this you have some kind of structure and routine in place already. Whether you recognise it and have developed it into a powerful, results producing, ally is the question in my mind. Have you?

Structure like this helps to improve performance and reduce the need to go into firefighting mode so often. This principle deserves some proper time and attention.

"If it's important – go and find out for yourself."
I sit in far too many meetings where statements are made as fact only to find out that they are half-truths or, worse, completely fictitious. I thank a former mentor for drilling this one into my head. When I was a young engineer I often ended up in conversations with the company's Global Projects Director, a person far more senior than myself. Luckily, I didn't take myself too seriously (as per the principle above) and enjoyed our conversations together, which usually took place while I fixed the software problems he seemed to regularly have / create.

His view, which I have certainly ratified too many times to ignore, was that most people won't bother to check themselves on the things that are important and instead build their decisions and views based on half-true and half-baked information. Therefore, if it is important, go and find out for yourself.

If you want to see the effect this approach can take, use the phrase 'great, I'll come and take a look' and often you can witness the activity that takes place just before you arrive. This is why quality checks, just before a contractor or supplier finishes doing whatever it is that they do for you, are so important. If you're going to personally take a look, and they know it, it will most likely be right (by the time you arrive). What gets measured certainly improves what gets managed.

Of course, I am not suggesting you check everything, I understand that you will have busy days to contend with. I am suggesting you invest the time for the handful of important things that are worth looking at, just to make sure that your plans will be on track when the next decision, or step in the plan, is undertaken.

This is not about the trust you have for your colleagues, this is about ensuring you have the right data to make decisions before you commit yourself to something, or make public declarations.

And, if it *is* about trust for you, then use the opportunity to support your staff to deliver on what they need to deliver, and then you can reduce your need to do so as they improve. There is a big difference between delegation and abdication and this principle supports effective delegation.

"Low value tasks are automated or eliminated."
If you have followed any of the Lean / Six Sigma movement over the last twenty years you will be acutely aware of the need to drive out low value activities from your business. In simple terms, anything that doesn't directly contribute to the value your business creates, needs to be nipped in the bud and either seriously throttled back or gotten rid of.

As managers we need to be even more aware of the impact we have in our businesses to create non-value adding tasks through the reporting requirements and meeting arrangements we organise. I am a big fan of formal reporting and formal meetings, but only if their impact (in terms of decision making and performance improvement) outweighs the burden to the business that they incur.

When it comes for us to look at the production and service delivery sides of our business, which is where many waste reduction activities seem to focus, the opportunity to eliminate waste is more obvious. We can see the various activities taking place that are in the wrong sequence for our value generation needs. The tweaking and tucking of our processes therefore seems to be directed at physical and visible activities.

When we go above this dotted line in our business' activities, into the management and leadership side of what we do, this spotting of opportunities for what we do seems less apparent to most of us. But, and this is the point, the same kinds of opportunities are sitting right before us. Every activity that we take part in during the days and weeks (as per your routine, see above) must offer some kind of support to the business' overall aim of creating value for its customers. If you review your routine activities (plus the recurring ad-hoc ones!) and ask yourself the following three questions you should be better armed to improve the efficiency and effectiveness of how your business works:

1. Do we actually need this activity?
2. How much time does the activity take?
3. What value does this activity offer our business?

Once you have the answers to those three questions you will have a view on what kinds of things can either be eliminated or minimised; if you can't get rid of it altogether then plan to find an easier and less intensive way of doing it.

Life changes and new issues come into the business. New managers join and have new requirements for running processes and reporting. Time moves on and we forget what we did before. This principle should sit at the heart of most businesses as we continually fight the fight for improved efficiency and effectiveness from our business activities.

"Reporting should be formal and informal (but not just one or the other)."

Getting the balance right between the formal reporting that is required for the management of the business and the informal reporting that allows for better teamwork and short-range results is a bit of an art.

Deciding on what reporting you want to have formally is a matter of planning. When you manage your business from a processes point of view you will find that the requirements for your reporting become quite straightforward. Ideally the purpose of your reporting is to provide information that either feeds another process in your business, or allows decision making to take place (for another process or another step in the same process). If some of your reporting doesn't help you to do either of these things then you may wish to re-consider the requirements for those reports, or cease their production.

The informal communication approach of your business may

be influenced by the location of offices, the seating arrangements of your staff, the company's culture around the use of email, canteen facilities and a whole array of other factors. The question that this principle provokes is 'do your staff talk to each other through the course of the day, or are they socially isolated?' The natural willingness for the team members to meet and speak, outside of the formal meetings and reporting channels, is something that should be observed and encouraged whenever possible.

This now becomes the challenge. If the staff meet regularly they might not see the need for the formal reporting and if it is not part of a management routine it could well be lost in the mix of day to day busy-ness. So, this principle is all about ensuring that your formal reporting is useful and that your informal communications are happening, and striving for an optimum balance of both approaches within your business.

"Walk don't run (think process and not headless chickens)."
This is the essence of this entire book, summarised as one principle. When you encounter a situation where the pace of your team has to change there is a good chance that there is a cape about to appear. Use this change in pace for two things:

1. Capture what the trigger / situation is, that is linked to the change in pace, as something that you need to go back to later to figure out how to eradicate it.
2. Stop (briefly) to look at your existing processes and ascertain if you can go back to your original pace through the better execution of your existing processes.

When we walk we are following our processes. When we run we increase the risk of flying out of the orbit of our processes. The worst situation is when we go 'feral' and run without any regard for our business' existing rules, procedures and processes. If you do have to run, because you need to wear a cape to fix whatever it is that needs to be fixed, take the opportunity to capture the situation for later on. When the dust has settled and you are able to reflect on the situation that ensued, look for the causes of the situation and put in place a permanent modification that will stop your business having to do the headless chicken dance (or put on a cape) for the same reason again.

"Concerns need to be shared, resolved and managed."
'Make do and mend' is a phrase that, in the right circumstances, is helpful. Put this into a process management perspective and it can be one of the most damaging things you can do in terms of productivity and performance. I actually heard a field technician use this phrase to justify not raising a concern with the business' processes. When I attended the meeting in question, and heard this comment it was a phrase used by most people in the business to condone poor performance. When we crunched the numbers behind his statement, to figure out the losses in the process, it pointed out a 50% time saving opportunity that was right under our noses. We all become disheartened if we get knocked back enough times. I get it. It is, however, up to us to raise our concerns to an appropriate person in the business, someone who can actually help us to deal with the issues, and get long lasting resolutions implemented.

Having a method to raise concerns in the first place is a good position to be in. A regular management meeting, a board in the production cell, a suggestion system, regular one to one meetings with your line manager... there isn't a shortage of ways to get your concerns raised.

The trick with these concerns (and by trick I should say there really is no trick) is to actually resolve the issue and manage out the change that needs to take place. Without the last two pieces of this puzzle it is perfectly understandable why people give up raising their concerns. It could be argued that raising concerns, in the wrong way, could be seen as complaining and that again is a challenge for us, as managers, to resolve. A constructive conversation about what is going on and what isn't working can take the improvements in business performance a long way.

Whatever your current situation is at work, making this principle one of your mantras is seriously worth considering.

Draw up your list and share it

During the past few pages I have shared with you a range of 'guiding principles' that both myself and my clients have found to be useful. I recommend that you mull over the list of principles and list out the ones that you think could be useful to your own day to day working. They are summarised below, for your reference:

- Data flows, it never stops.
- Production is always planned and appropriate targets are set.
- Preparation equals productivity.
- Take pride in the workplace.
- Lead by example.
- Take your work seriously, but not yourself (or others).
- Routines are established and maintained.
- If it's important – go and find out for yourself.
- Low value tasks are automated or eliminated.
- Reporting should be formal and informal (but not just one or the other).
- Walk don't run (think process and not headless chickens).
- Concerns need to be shared, resolved and managed.

I'm sure that you also have your own mantras that serve you. And, like the one I picked up from one of my mentors, there are probably good ones you have heard from other people that you could adopt also.

Draw up a list of the handful (five to ten is a good quantity to have) of guiding principles you have shortlisted and use it to help with your own personal performance around process management.

When you feel comfortable, share the list with your team. Explain the reasons for sharing it (to help drive the right kind of cape crushing behaviours the business needs) and find ways to talk about the list regularly. When you get crises occurring in the business you can also use the list as a way to reflect quickly upon which principle wasn't followed and it should accelerate your decision making when it comes to making changes in your business.

Guiding principles are a great way to change behaviours and start to eradicate the need to wear a cape so often. To accelerate this, let us move on to review ways to spot the cape in your business.

Action Points

- Pull apart the list of principles that I shared above and select that ones that fit with how you want to operate your business.
- Add in other guiding principles / productive truths that will help your team to orientate themselves when the going gets tough.
- Communicate the principles to your team, and what they are for, and keep copies of the principles in prominent locations.

How to Spot the Cape

Now that you have gotten this far in the book I am hoping that you have a clear picture of where and when the cape appears in your business. But, hope is never a great strategy so let me run through some key areas from general business life where the cape can appear. As you go through this section have a think about your business and which examples come to mind that you can focus on and tackle first.

Do you know who wears the cape?

A great place to start with the spotting of capes is by person, after all it is a person that has to wear a cape!

Are there people in your business who seem to leap into action more often than others?

Are these people fixing their own issues, or other peoples?
The person we are looking for is the person who has to wear the cape in order to keep the business on track. If you look around your business you will likely see a core group of cape wearers, keep them in your mind as we progress through this book. You will need to engage these people, in order to help change their perspective, which we will look at in the next chapter.

What are your repeat failures?

Within most businesses, when this kind of reactive

troubleshooting is taking place on a regular basis, there will be patterns of activity. There will be themes and periodic episodes, that when you step back and look at the history of your business, you will see crop up time and time again.

If you can't think of any themes, try adjusting your focus and look for the common thread of the issues your business has faced instead. To do this you may need to look at the business in a slightly more generic way and look for the gist of the problem and not get tied up with the specifics. The precise same problem might not happen, but the general issue may well be popping its head up on a regular basis. One of my clients used to treat each delivery failure to its customer as a discreet incident, but when you stood back it was clear that they had a general problem with the packing instructions being supplied to the Despatch department in the business. They treated each failure as if it were a new experience, but the reality was that it was the same old thing happening again and again and again.

Make a note of where your repeating failures are taking place in your business and, if possible, try to determine what generic issue is causing these failures. If you think back to the idea of 'cause and effect' you will realise that the aim here is to figure out what is causing the general effect and plan to eliminate that. Again, I'll share some tools and approaches to help you do this. The point here is that you will need to identify some targets to go after in order to stop the repeating pattern from occurring.

Where are the pressure points in your business?

No business is perfect and they all have their weaknesses.

What are they in your business?

Identifying the weaknesses is a simple way to create some more targets to aim for and, again, it might be helpful to describe these in generic terms. If we get bogged down with the details of specific situations for too long this identification of pressure points can seem too difficult. Stepping back from the detail to get a bigger picture and assess the overall situation is a good strategy to employ periodically, and this is one of those times.

Some examples from my past working life of pressure points / weaknesses in both my clients and my employers (before we sorted them out!) include:
- An inability to capacity plan workloads (leading to projects being delivered late).
- A lack of visibility over debts (leading to cashflow issues).
- Poor communication with suppliers (leading to late start of production).
- An ineffective working knowledge of office software and systems (leading to inefficient working practices).
- A lack of focus on following through on ideas and promises (leading to disengagement within the workforce).

...and you get the picture. Being aware of your key business weaknesses allows you to home in and identify cape creating situations that you can focus on and plan to avoid in the future.

Take a short time out from reading this and identify one or two weaknesses that are present in your business and make a note of them.

Start to prioritise

One of our biggest challenges, when we start to look at improving our businesses, is to decide where to start.

Now that you have:
- identified some pressure points in your business,
- clarified who your key cape wearers are,
- drafted a vision for improving,
- a list of current issues you want to resolve and,
- guiding principles that you want to embrace,
it becomes imperative that you come up with a priority to work to. Too many improvement projects fall over because the people working on them have been spread too thin. Our ambitions to eradicate the cape need to be in line with our capacity and capability to do so.

If improvement projects are new to you it might be sensible to prioritise your improvement projects based on their complexity and ability to generate results in the short term. This is not to say that you shouldn't be ambitious, I am suggesting that if you are new to coaxing colleagues to undertake changes, and iterating your approach so that you actually realise the results you want, then prioritising on this basis makes sense.

If you are more seasoned at making changes a reality then you might look at your priorities differently. Looking at the needs of the business you might see a logical progression through the improvement areas that can help you to generate your priority sequence.

If you are struggling to pick a number one for your list (because who doesn't want to have all of the results right now and all at once?) then ask yourself this question:

"If I could only work on one improvement, which one would it be?"

It might take a little time to figure out your priority sequence, but remembering these two facts may help you to decide what is most important:

1. Not all improvements are equal, some will deliver greater results for your business than others. Find the 'biggest bang for your buck'.

2. If you stretch yourself (or your team) too thin, or confuse yourself (or, again, your team) by having too much on the go, you will grind the results of your improvements to a halt and lose momentum entirely.

Even worse, if you don't come up with a priority and you get a little lost with your improvements you will potentially create more cape wearing episodes that could have been avoided. To get buy in from your team you ideally want to have some small, quick, wins that you can publicise. You can build upon this trickle of successes, so that you can tackle the bigger projects (that will inevitably need more involvement from your team). Do not lose momentum!

As you improve your business' ability to deliver change and handle more complicated changes (what may seem complicated today may seem simple in a few months' time) the number of projects you can deliver at any one time can increase. If this is something that you are wondering about at the moment, take some solace in knowing that it is far better to start off with one project being delivered brilliantly and accelerating progress rather than starting off with too many and slowly having to ramp progress down as you realise that you're not getting anywhere.

One of my clients had this very same problem; their eagerness to improve was blinding their sense of reason when it came to scheduling their changes. This was a business that showed poor disciplines in many areas of their business, had several members of staff that wore capes almost permanently and failed to communicate even the most basic of information to their colleagues and team members. My insistence that one small project was the right place to start was agreed to initially, but as soon as I stepped out of the business their enthusiasm took over and another four projects were added to the roster immediately. As you can imagine, their business performance turned ugly and I started to receive a number of phone calls. We went back to just one simple project and channelled their enthusiasm in the right way so that this one improvement was delivered properly. I love enthusiasm, but when it isn't put into the right places at the right time it can cause havoc! Bear this in mind when you get going with your improvements.

So, if you have your prioritised cape eliminating / business improvement projects let's move on to having the kinds of conversations that get change happening.

Action Points

- Draw up a shortlist of the most frequent cape wearers in your business and keep an eye on how they operate.

- Draw up a list of the pressure points in your business and keep an eye on how well they are working.
- Prioritise both lists to ensure your time and support is being directed to the most important areas.

Starting an Ongoing Conversation

Improving a business is not always a straightforward affair... if it was you probably wouldn't be reading this book. For me, nothing happens (in terms of improving) without a conversation. If you want to rid your business of the capes that it contains you definitely need to speak to your people!

This section of the book looks at getting conversations going and how to use these dialogues to propel the strategies that are still to come.

It's all about the people

No matter how good you are at designing how your business should work, it means nothing if the people in the business aren't engaged enough to execute the business' processes in the right way. There isn't a week that goes past where I don't use the phrase:

"we don't need more processes, we need more execution"

Is that the same for you?

I am a big believer that the majority of people can perform well under the right conditions; a good working environment, pro-active managers, good processes and enough support / education. If you have all of these things and you are still facing problems by the time you have tried out the ideas in this book then it might be the case that your business and the person / people in question aren't a good fit for each other.

Finding out where your people are in this mix of factors can come out from talking to them about what is going on generally in the business, hence the importance of this chapter. Skills matrices and past appraisals all have their place, but a general conversation about how their part of the business is working can often reveal a great deal without having to follow a rigid interview structure. I have worked with many people that had been written off by others, but once I had found out that they either didn't understand or didn't know how a specific business process was meant to operate I could do something about it. And, guess what? Fewer capes for me to deal with thereafter…

Group discussions and one-to-ones

Like all things improvement you can approach the need for conversations in a number of ways. The two simplest concepts to consider are one to ones and group discussions.

One to ones work especially well if you have someone who can seriously impact the business, such as a senior manager or an influential member of staff, and you don't want to dilute their thoughts and opinions.

Group working, on the other hand, is useful when you want to cover more people and they are all working toward a common goal (such as is the case when you have a department coming together to make a change project happen). As I said earlier, this is about having a conversation so your group can't be too big. Anything larger than eight people (including yourself) is likely to kill the ability to have a meaningful multi-way discussion.

Understanding how the conversation is flowing is important to gauge when you are in these conversations, to ensure that both you and the other people in the discussion are getting enough 'air time' to get their ideas and questions raised. Thinking this through before you start your conversations is worthwhile, you may choose to split groups up, combine groups or have one-to-ones when you reflect on who will be in the discussions. Troublesome individuals, or those that hog the air time, might be best left for one-to-one discussions.

Getting the conversation started

So, where do you start when it comes to having a conversation of this nature?

At this point in the book we have already covered a few points, haven't we?
- You may have a utopian future to consider.
- You may have a selection of 'guiding principles' to discuss.
- You may have a list of pressure points, or recent incidents, that you can bring to the table.

Setting the scene by discussing the issues that the business is facing, stating that you want to eliminate re-active (cape wearing) efforts and asking for their input is all that needs to happen to get a conversation going. Once you have got this out in the open then you can get started with the meat of the conversation.

If you aren't in the habit of writing agendas for meetings, please take this as an opportunity to do so and identify a handful of topics to discuss in your first meeting. The output from your first meeting is likely to fuel your future meetings (especially in terms of following up on the subsequent actions that you agree during the meetings) and eventually you may come up with a standard agenda for your meetings thereafter.

Building improvement relationships

You might be excited at the opportunity of discussing improvement ideas openly with your team. They might be dreading it.

When you do meet for the first time, as a group, to discuss eliminating the capes from your business you may need to clarify how these conversations will be handled.

Some pointers to bear in mind include:
- We are here to experiment with ideas;
- Bringing incomplete solutions to the table is OK;
- We're not here to belittle each other;
- Piloting and investigation is to be the aim of the team;
- You won't be putting the business at risk (because of the ideas being ratified and trialled before anything serious happens).

Conversations like these are exploratory in nature. The answers aren't known (otherwise we wouldn't be needing to have the discussions in the first place) and reassuring the people in the conversations that this is the case is the first step to making the conversations productive. To some degree everyone in the conversation is on the same level. The idea that you are their boss in this conversation is null and void. You are there to facilitate the discussions about how your business needs to lose the various capes people have to wear day to day and how you can all test out ideas and tighten up what happens with your business processes so that the need for capes reduces over time.

As your time in these conversations continues, you have the opportunity to find out more about what makes your colleagues tick and there is the good chance that you can develop better working relationships with those around you. Better working relationships have the potential to improve business performance in their own right and therefore shouldn't be overlooked.

Sharing and learning

To foster the learning and exploratory nature of these conversations it is vital that there is an open forum to share what has been learned and how these ideas can be applied across different parts of the business. I mentioned earlier that these conversations shouldn't put the business at risk and I think this is the right time to expand on that point further.

I have found that many people have great ideas that they can share generally in the business, but are either shy or concerned that they will look foolish or fear risking the business in some way. For example, if you proposed a change to the sequence in the way that you accept work into your business and made a wholesale change and it didn't work, then you would possibly put the business at risk; customers might be annoyed and sales might drop. If we take the basic idea proposed and create a pilot change to test out the idea then the risk will be reduced.

The basic cycle is therefore:
1. Generate an idea.
2. Create a mini version of the idea.

3. Deliver a pilot / test for the mini version.
4. Review the results produced.
5. Expand on the mini pilot project, or change the test.
6. Deliver the next version of your project.
7. Repeat the steps 4 through to 6 until you roll out the idea fully.

This is a combination of the PDCA (Plan, Do, Check, Act) cycle borrowed from Lean production with the Kaizen idea of taking tiny steps to gain confidence and experience. You take a tiny step and give it a whirl, if you like the results you can do a bigger and better version and keep repeating this approach until you have a full-blown transformation on your hands!

There is a downloadable reference to this approach (and how to get the most out of the PDCA cycle) that you can view on the website:

To access the PDCA 'tip sheet', to help you implement change effectively, visit the downloads page via the Links chapter.

Making this habitual

As with all changes it can be hard to be consistent and ensure that these conversations keep going. There is a great tendency that, when you start winning at the process of change, you then start to take your foot off the pedal and actually slow down to the point where any gains made have been lost. This doesn't even take into account that most of us have day jobs, that are already demanding on our time.

The phenomenon of taking our foot of the gas once we get going, however, happens with all kinds of changes. There are many pressures on businesses and once an improvement gets traction and looks like it might actually pull off the results it is designed for, people often relax. It might look like it is a sure thing now, but unless we carry on and see the improvement through to the correct end point, it isn't a sure thing.

I remember working with a business that had a real problem with their order book backlog. Every few months the backlog would get to a level that would see the senior executives of the business descend from their offices and get involved with their production teams. They would lead the discussions for their 'arrears reduction plan' and stay involved until some progress to reduce the level had taken effect. After they left, the progress would be maintained for a short period of time and the results would continue to improve also. Then, like clockwork, another issue would become prevalent in the business and require the team focussing on the arrears reduction to change their focus and look into this new issue.

You've guessed it, the arrears would then start to creep up and the cycle would then start again in a few months' time.
As a side note – this situation only resolved itself when we approached the problem using some of the methods described in this book and we had a frank discussion about the cycle they experienced. The business decided to put fewer resources into the resolution of the arrears problem, but in a way that was sustainable; they were happy to experience slower, but permanent, results. Fundamentally, they had to change a couple of their working practices and modify one of their business processes (once they had control over the situation) and this prevented them from relapsing into a serious backlog problem again.

Shifting your focus from dealing with one problem and then moving to another potentially harmful situation is one that we all have to deal with. This is a universal issue that must be dealt with by every business and the question we need to ask ourselves is 'how do I insulate our improvement conversation from this same effect?'

A very simple strategy that I have used, and that my clients have also used, is to piggy-back existing meetings that are already routine within the business. Or, put another way, we can extend existing business habits to form new habits. Of course, you don't want to jeopardise your existing good habits, but finding something where you already have the right people in the right place at the same time is a good way to ensure that you can keep your conversations and activities moving forward.

Another strategy that works well is to have the discussion as one of the first items of activity in the working day. If you subscribe to Parkinson's Law (that work expands to fill the time available) then you can use this approach to great effect. The discussions don't have to take up a lot of time once you have had the initial chat (which always seems to take a lot of time, understandably). If this approach is new to you and your business you might need to be firm with others for the first couple of meetings. People will be trying to get out of the conversation because of other pressing issues that are facing the business (cape wearing episodes most likely!), but it is essential that the right kinds of disciplines and expectations are maintained as this is the kind of working style that will support losing the capes longer term. If you intentionally keep your discussions short then you will be able to still deal with your business issues in a timely manner, and this strategy for keeping your conversations ongoing becomes viable.

Similarly, there may be an ideal time in the working week where your team is quieter. It doesn't matter when and where you have your discussions, as long as you find a slot that is sustainable.

Don't let the conversation stop

So, let's say that you have found a slot in your week that you can use to turn this dialogue into an ongoing activity, so that it becomes a habit. Let's also say that you are making clear progress with your improvements, that your team is enjoying the process of change and that your business is starting to witness the benefits of the activity.

What do you do when you come to the end of the improvement you are talking about?

Your team should be growing in confidence as you move from the pilot stage through to a full-blown change. Why would you want to let them leave this conversation now? You have invested in them and have grown them in terms of their effectiveness and their ability to deliver results as part of this journey. The answer should be simple then, shouldn't it? You have the opportunity to move them on to the next priority in your list of improvement activities.

After the first improvement success, you may need to re-arrange the team and possibly add or exchange team members, depending on their skills and appropriateness for supporting the subsequent projects. You may wish to create sub-teams and tackle more than one improvement at a time.

As a cautionary note, please bear in mind that the more improvement projects you undertake at any one time can have a near exponential impact on your resources. Add in more concurrent improvement activities only if your eyes are wide open (in terms of the staff you have available to undertake the work). This doesn't even take into account any additional finances you may need to make the improvement come to life, but whatever the burden is on your business, tread carefully when you start to increase your rate of change.

Transformations need actions

When you are holding your discussions with your team, it is vital that you are able to effectively capture the actions from your discussions and manage them through to their conclusions. The actions that you capture will essentially be the focus of your activity going forward. I see too many businesses fail at this point, and lose out on experiencing meaningful changes taking place in the organisation. The following pointers will help you to ensure that you don't do the same thing. The goal of this book is to help you find ways to eliminate the unnecessary cape wearing that goes on in your business and good management of your action plans is core to this.

- Ensure that your actions are clear and understood by the person that they are assigned to.
- Agree on completion dates that are achievable (or frustration will kick in all too soon) and don't leave them open ended.
- Only have one person responsible for each action point. The person who undertakes the work may be someone different, but only one person can be responsible.
- Leave space on your action plan for comments and updates so that each action's status is clear.
- Include the status of each action on your plan; 'live', 'complete' and 'on-hold' should be enough for most businesses.
- Keep your improvement plans separate; if you have three projects then have three action plans.

- Know how many improvement projects you can operate at any one time, based on their complexity, duration and involvement. If in doubt – stick to one at a time.
- Have your action plans in a visible location; physically stick them up on the walls so that everyone can see them. A meeting room used for your routine operations meetings is a great place to host your plans. Hiding your action plans (such as on a server) is a sure-fire way to limit the rate of progress that can be made.
- If you have a new idea for a new improvement project then start to capture the actions as soon as you can. The status of the project may be that it is in a queue (so that you don't overload your business with improvement activity). Work out how you prioritise your improvement projects and launch it when another one concludes.
- Exert your right to change the mix of your improvement projects if something more pressing comes along, but do so with the knowledge that chopping and changing your improvements can have a detrimental effect in terms of both morale and results. Clutch projects in and out of being active in a controlled manner, if you have to.
- Update your action plans regularly and consider assigning responsibilities to your staff in terms of who is responsible for updating which plan.

If you apply the above to your improvement actions you should find that your ability to close out the actions and make meaningful improvements will increase.

In the next section, we shall look at what is, in my opinion, an underused approach to launching improvement projects, and an approach that you can use to great effect to ensure that your action plans are focused on eliminating capes and delivering the precise results that you want.

Action Points

- Decide who you want to speak to about improvement and cape reduction, how and at what frequency.
- Arrange a practical meeting slot, so that you can keep a conversation going for the longer term.
- Ensure the conversations are two-way and capture any learning points or actions that come out from them.
- Use this dialogue as a way to share ideas and to accelerate the rate of change taking place in your business.

Worthy Challenges and PIDs

Now that you have some conversations started in your business, and you already have some actions to be undertaken, it is time to think about the next step in this journey.

People often respond to 'worthy challenges'

Having 'worthy challenges' can help take someone from being a chronic cape wearer to a staunch advocate of proper process management. For many people just becoming aware of the costs, effort and strain of having to constantly delve into reactive fire-fighting (aka cape wearing) mode is enough to let them want to make positive changes. For this group it is more important to offer a road map of how they can get out of this situation, enabling them to join your quest.

For others, there is the distinct possibility that wearing a cape is a large part of their identity and the idea of having fewer cape moments in the business is unpalatable. I know of several cape advocates who have left businesses after their major (repeating) problems disappeared quoting the reasons for leaving as the 'job is no longer fun'. This will continue to happen, the question to ask is 'is the business here to serve customers and make a profit, or provide entertainment for my staff?'

From the conversations that have now been taking place you will possibly have found some of the 'hot buttons' with the people who end up wearing capes more often. Assuming that they want to stay, you may be able to use your insights into their motivation to provide them with a different way to have esteem and identity within the business. You could give them a worthy challenge to help them focus their energy and skills!

Being the best...

One of the best worthy challenges is to invite the person you are going to focus on to become the best at what it is they do. For example, if you have a designer (that doesn't follow protocol) their worth challenge may be to become the best designer in the world. You can insert any job role into that sentence:

To become the best 'job role' in the world.

For many people this requires a narrowing of their focus, to become intimate with every aspect of their job (including the procedures and processes that surround the job). Doing less better is a great strategy that most of us can adopt generally, but in this sense, it is an opportunity to stop looking at the distractions that surround us and really home in on the nuances of our own tasks.

To be able to do this you will need to have a few ingredients ready before you even try to have this conversation, they are:
- An idea of what the utopia future looks like.
- The benefit of this person stepping up and becoming the best in the world (the 'why').
- Some cape wearing examples to put your request into context.
- The general business' decision to move away from re-active cape wearing situations and moving into

proactive process management (with occasional cape wearing only).

-   Clarity as to the inputs and outputs this person has to deal with.

If you have worked your way systematically through this book you will likely have most of the ingredients already. Additional to this list will be your knowledge of this individual and how best to handle this conversation.

Being crystal clear – the PID

A PID is a Project Initiation Document, a tool used across many different business sectors. I can only go by my feel for how widely used PIDs are, but my feeling is that they are still an underused approach, with many business favouring the 'leap into action with no plan and hope for the best' strategy instead.

The purpose of taking the time out to write up a PID is to ensure that everyone involved with a project (but specifically the person / team delivering the project and the customers / stakeholders) knows exactly what they are getting into.

Going back to my example earlier about the designer becoming the best designer in the world, it would be good to agree what the outcome of this activity looks like before the work commences – wouldn't you agree?

I have seen far too many projects reach their conclusion only to find out that the primary customer of the project didn't feel that the project had delivered any meaningful content. I remember on a specific project where the owner of the company told his project team about all of the things that they hadn't delivered on. These were items that were not obvious to anyone on the team (or myself, as an observer) and were nonetheless defined as the must have deliverables. I'm sure that you are thinking that if these items were defined at the outset then there wouldn't have been a problem, and you are right.

Elements of a PID

A PID can take many formats, but all have many common features including:
-   The title of your project.
-   The key people involved with the project. Be sure to include any stakeholders that are interested / affected by the project.
-   The problem (or opportunity) being addressed by this project.
-   A high-level description of the project, how it solves the issue / problem faced.
-   Start dates and end dates.
-   Clarification of the deliverables of the project - what are people going to experience (see, feel, hear) when the project is concluded? As per the example above, this part is critical.
-   How will you measure if the project has been a success? You may be able to tie this into any existing business Key Performance Indicators, or create specific measures / achievements for this project.
-   What is in scope for this project? Where does the project's boundaries start and end? This helps to clarify where you will be putting your efforts.

- What is out of scope for the project? This point goes hand in hand with the 'in scope' element, it is often advantageous to clarify what isn't included. If there are specific hot topics in the business that aren't being addressed as part of this project spell them out here.
- The benefits should be detailed and really reflect any business case (if one has been done already) and summarise all of the good business reasons to do the project.
- Any risks that might be associated with the project need to be identified, that need to be considered and taken into account, before the project is signed off.
- How the progress and status of the project will be reported during its life.
- Finally, the PID will need to include a section for the key project personnel, customers and stakeholders where they can sign off the project (once signed you're good to go!).

To access a free PID template, to tailor to meet your own business' needs, visit the downloads page via the Links chapter.

Launching the project

Once you have completed all of the main elements in your PID, you can now get the project signed off (see the final section of the downloadable template).

To launch the project, it is often best to have a meeting with all of the key people (who need to sign the document) in order to ensure clarity as to what the project is (and isn't) meant to do, how the reporting will work and what will be achieved as an outcome.

When the meeting's participants have arrived at an agreement about the above points, the document can be signed and the project formally initiated. If the contents of the PID need to be altered, do it as quickly as possible and get the document signed before people have forgotten about the project and need to reconvene to discuss it again.

The promotion of the project to the wider audience of the business can then ensue and it is vital in the context of what you are trying to achieve with this book - to reinforce the message about reducing the level of re-active efforts that are taking place in the business (aka the capes). By layering the messages cascading through the business, about the aim of the improvements being to reduce the amount of cape wearing required by the business' personnel, you will be able to accelerate the rate of improvement activity. This type of work will become normal over time, accepted as being what you do in your business and break down some of the barriers around people engaging with the change process.

In essence, that is what all of these efforts are trying to do. We are aiming for a 'business as usual' that is process driven, with strong effective management, and only an occasional need for having to use our superhero strengths to run about and patch up the cracks in our business.

Let's not get carried away!

If you are new to the idea of launching projects in a formal manner then let me just heed a word of caution… as I have already mentioned, too many projects at once may tip your improvement activities over and you may never get to see the level of change you have been planning (or hoping!) for. All of us have a natural capacity for juggling our workloads. Too many change projects can stop us from delivering anything at all, the complete opposite of what is wanted. To compound matters, the more change projects that you undertake at the same time, the more head scratching, experimenting, waiting, asking and hypothesising you may have to do.

Remember, if the change was easy to make you would probably have done it already. So, logic implies that what you want to do won't necessarily be easy. That said, some improvements will require less effort and will be implemented successfully with fewer attempts and less overall efforts. Some will be complete nightmares in comparison.

So, what's the answer?

In the first instance I would recommend that you start with just one improvement focus. Prioritise undertaking one improvement only and focus on that activity until you have a solid improvement in place. By 'solid' I mean that it is firmly embedded into the business and has become part of the normal day-to-day activities. It has become an effective habit.

If you are currently in the midst of improvements and feel that you are getting nowhere, you can apply the same approach and pare back your activities until you find your optimum balance. And remember, if in doubt – do less better!

Sometimes it isn't clear what we need to be working on to get a proper change to happen for our business; changes get made and still the same kinds of problems occur. If this is something that is happening to you then it is time for us to examine the root cause behind our issues...

Action Points

- Download the PID template and tailor it to suit your business' needs.
- Experiment with the format by either specifying a new project, or re-specifying a project that is struggling.
- Communicate the PID approach with your teams, if you choose to trial it in your business.

Let's Get to the Root

Core to the idea of losing the cape is the idea of fixing fundamental issues that are lying behind the issues we see day to day. If you can cast your mind back to my overview of 'cause and effect' thinking, the challenge comes to truly understand what is the ultimate cause of the effects we are experiencing.

What's behind the need for the cape?

Often the cause is obvious and we can quickly eliminate the problems we are suffering from by making a simple change. I would expect that most of the changes you make to your business will be quite straightforward; being aware of the capes present in your business is often the biggest step forward.

However, there will be instances when you have tried to make changes and yet the problems you come across will keep on re-appearing. It's at times like this that you will really need to dig under the skin of your business to figure out what is triggering these repeat episodes.

Getting to the root of your problems

You have most likely heard the phrase 'root cause problem solving' during your working life. However, I find that there are relatively few people who can persevere and get to the bottom of the problems faced by their business and put in place a long lasting (if not permanent) solution to the problem.

I don't think that this is an art form to master, but it is certainly a way of thinking that seems to lend itself to some people and not others. When you reach the root of your issues a certain simplicity and clarity will appear and this will allow you to make some far reaching changes to your business. The really good news is that, when you reach the true root causes behind your issues, the solutions are often very simple - disarmingly so!

I feel that time is one of the biggest factors for this approach not being effectively deployed. People are under pressure to deliver on their day jobs and taking time out to find the true root cause may seem like a luxury. If only these people could weigh up the chronic cost of living with their capes versus the relatively small amount of time root cause problem solving takes...

Why, why, why, why, why?

The technique I want to share with you is a (slightly) structured version of the five why root cause problem solving approach.

The most basic description of this method is to keep on asking 'why?' questions to the people involved with a project / process / problem until you reach the root cause. On my travels I see people literally ask 'why?' in quick succession and then get frustrated when they don't generate any meaningful results. The explanation I will give later in this section is designed to arm you with a way to more consistently achieve better results using this method.

When I get involved with my client's root cause problem solving this is my preferred approach. The conversations that go alongside the 'five why' method can often lead to other interesting insights and opportunities. Beware! The aim of the exercise is to solve the puzzle in front of you, not to get lost. If you embrace this approach and find other interesting avenues of enquiry to improve your business, make a note of them and come back to them later.

To summarise the power of this approach, I have worked with clients who have been completely lost with regards how to improve their business. They seemed to have so many problems facing their business that it was unclear to them where to begin. The 'five why' method has an amazing ability to cut through the noise of business problems and direct you to the tackling of a handful of basic, fundamental, business issues where the solutions are usually in your direct control.

Getting tricked by the symptoms

A common failure that I see when people attempt to find a root cause (using this method, or any other root cause problem solving method) is that they stop too early. As we discussed, the objective of the 'five why' approach is to determine the true root cause. When the questioning process is enacted it can be tempting for the people taking part to claim that they have reached a satisfactory conclusion when in fact they haven't.

For example, I have seen many people reach the conclusion that their processes would be better if they delivered more training to their staff. It is a harder pill to swallow to say that the real cause is weak management and a lack of good habits within the leadership team of the business. I said before that the root cause should lead you to a simple solution, but not necessarily an easy solution.

Don't let yourself get tricked by the high-level symptoms of the problem; keep going until you reach a point in your exploration where you can truly say that if you resolved the current (why) reason that the problem would disappear altogether. If you think that the problem could find a way to resurface (in the sense that the remedy of the reason you are at would not completely resolve the problem) then you need to keep digging.

I think you have the point now, so let me get on with explaining the structured approach to using the 'five why' method.

Capture the 'who', the 'where' and the 'when'

As you identify some cape wearing issues to resolve, based on the key people and key pressure points in your business, it can be helpful to ensure that they are articulated in as simple language as possible. Simply stated targets help others to understand the issues at hand and will help you get off to a good start when you implement your changes.

My background is in engineering and during that time I was taught a soul-less version of the Rudyard Kipling poem "I Keep Six Honest Serving Men ...", which begins with the verse:

I KEEP six honest serving-men
(They taught me all I knew);
Their names are What and Why and When
And How and Where and Who.
I send them over land and sea,

I send them east and west;
But after they have worked for me,
I give them all a rest.

The version I learned, however, was called 5W1H and stands
for:
- What
- Why
- When
- Where
- Who
- How

I suggest that when you are stating your targets for cape
reduction you use all of these sub-headings, except for 'why'
(which I will explain in a moment). Try and convert your
observations and insights about what needs to be looked into
first using these prompts and see if you can articulate your
issues in a way that can be understood by all. When you get it
right there will be fewer queries and misunderstandings and it
will make your life easier in the long haul. When the right
description is given about the issues to be overcome, you will
experience a simpler problem solving process and the
implementation of an easier change project.

Going back to the earlier example of the capacity planning
pressure point:
- What – We don't have a capacity planning tool to
  accept work into the business.
- When – It occurs each time we accept an order into the
  business, during a meeting that takes place at 9am each
  morning.
- Where – The order acceptance takes place in the main
  meeting room.

- Who – The Sales Manager, the Production Manager, the Engineering Manager, the Purchasing Manager and the Planner attend the meeting.
- How – A standard agenda is followed, alongside the use of a computer to refer to business data.

In this example I now have the main elements of my target identified, but the critical 'why?' question now needs to be asked.

Thinking about the true cause

This goes right back to our review of the 'cause and effect' thinking required to figure out how we change our results. The question (from 5W1H) that I have not mentioned yet is the 'why?' question. Asking this question allows you to hop down from the current level of enquiry to the next level down (as you head to what is commonly known as the 'root cause'). Asking good why questions can require patience as you get the hang of asking the right kinds of questions. It can take some practice to be able to ask really effective questions to help you dig down to what is really going on, but the payoff is worth it. Use the statements you have made to form a why question (e.g. why does this issue arise despite having the senior management team present in the meeting?).

This approach is known as the 'five why' approach as it is widely recognised that you can get to the root cause of most issues within five why based questions. The approach that works really well is to continue to use the 'what, when, where, how, who' questions to find out the information you need in order to ask a really good 'why' question. You repeat this process, of digging around and then asking a great why question, until you hit an 'aha!' moment. You'll know when you have hit this point because you will have a flash of the blindingly obvious and see a really clear cause-and-effect relationship.

If you find the solution to be embarrassingly simple don't worry, this is quite normal! We can get so stuck in our day to day activities that the blindingly obvious can get missed. This is why we often have to wear the cape, we can't see the wood for the trees (as the popular saying goes!).

I am not going to go further into this technique as I believe that practice is the best teacher for this approach. There are just three things I want you to keep in mind as you try out this questioning approach:
- Ask intelligently (not just blurting out the word why).
- Ask politely (we want answers, not fear of punishment).
- Keep going until you have an 'aha!' moment.

Pushing five why to its absolute conclusion

If you give up prematurely when you try out the 'five why' approach you will most likely not reach a satisfying conclusion. You will dig up something meaningful only if you persist to the 'aha!' moment and have a flash of the blindingly obvious.

If you dig a little way you will be able to reduce the severity of the cape wearing episodes. If you dig further than this you will see a drop in the number of capes that need to be worn. If you get to the bottom of the matter you will have the best chance of eliminating the need for capes altogether for this particular issue facing your business.

A client of mine once had problems with the quality of their products when produced by various shifts. We employed the 'five why' method to find out why this situation was occurring. It was a regular cape wearing exercise for the business and the team selected to deal with this issue were unsure where to start. That is the beauty of 'five why', you can start pretty much anywhere and get to where you need to get to. In this particular case, however, the team got to a really good conclusion. They came up with a simple solution that would stop the quality issues from arising on their shifts and then the question was asked – "how far can you push this thinking?"

The team struggled to probe and answer two more 'why?' questions pertaining to this string of exploration but came up with a stunning answer that identified a very simple link they could create in their business that would not only crush the cape in question, but improve the efficiency and effectiveness of their internal training programmes whilst synchronising production with the commercial side of the business. The people involved were gobsmacked that they had identified such a brilliant improvement for the business and one that was simple to implement and manage.

That is the power of digging down to the root of the issue and the very reason why it is worth practising this technique until you get the hang of it. Not only can you quickly find ways to get rid of the capes in your business, but it engages your team and has the potential to identify huge business improvements that are sitting right under your nose!

Making changes is one thing when it comes to losing the cape, but how you manage and measure life after the change is key to sustaining the benefits. This is the topic for our next chapter.

Action Points

- Find some ongoing business issues that you want to eradicate and use them to practice the 'five why' method.
- Become skilled at asking the right kinds of questions and improve the results you get from using this method.
- Share the technique and train your colleagues, so that this approach can be used naturally as part of the normal working day.

Habits, Outputs and Reporting

If I could pinpoint one factor that really impacts on a business' need to wear capes, it would be their habits. There has been lots written on the subject of habits; for many they seem to be an elusive component of success. But, being an engineer by profession, I see habits as the ingrained result of having a formalised (business) routine. The two other factors mentioned in the title of this chapter (outputs and reporting) arise from having the right kinds of habits and we shall look at taking advantage of these three things so that you can reduce the surprises happening inside your business.

What are your business' bad habits?

Before I get into the 'how to' elements of this section, let me pose the above question to you first.

Does your business have known bad habits?

I'm guessing that when you looked at the utopian view of your business you didn't include any bad habits on your list. Most businesses have some kind of bad habits already present that you will need to be conscious of; bad habits affect the general discipline of a business and is another factor that can lead to more cape wearing moments.

Bad habits I am thinking of include:
- Not starting meetings on time.
- Starting new working practices and dropping them shortly afterwards.
- Ignoring management requests.

- Changing standard working practices without agreement.
- Making decisions on behalf of others without them knowing.

And the list goes on…

Knowing what some of the bad habits are, and identifying their root cause, and coming up with a plan to eliminate (or at least alleviate – we are human after all!) is a good place to start, before you go on to define some really effective habits that your business could benefit from.

Do you have a routine?

So, the most obvious question that comes to mind now is:

"Does your business have a routine already?"

Routines drive all kinds of business activity. Some routines are formalised, visible and managed; some are unspoken habits.

Being clear about the routines that are undertaken in your business are is key to figuring out if the little tasks (at cause) - that can make all the difference to the results (the effect) - are being completed frequently enough, to the right standard and in a timely manner.

I'm sure that you hear the phrase 'I don't have time to complete these tasks' in your business. There appears to always be someone, somewhere, that makes this comment. Over the years my observation around this comment is that whilst these individuals don't have time to complete these seemingly small tasks, they do have time for the significant levels of fire-fighting and rework (or, cape wearing activities) that need to take place. It is a challenge of all managers to help their staff to see the relationship between cause and effect that can make a difference.

As I write this section of the book I recall a conversation I had just yesterday with a manager who was grumbling about having to 'tick the boxes' by completing a formal planning activity. We reviewed the work that had been completed and discussed what came out from doing the exercise. The raft of management actions that the planning spawned were all designed to prevent failure later on in the project and improve the overall efficiency, effectiveness and profit of the project (as well as customer delight!). The manager couldn't disagree with the usefulness of the process, but hadn't put two and two together prior to our conversation. We discussed what risks the business would face if the exercise wasn't completed on a regular basis and I'm pleased to say that the penny dropped.

Similarly, I can recall a situation about ten years ago where a series of routine checks were not being performed by a purchasing office in a business. Late material deliveries and frantic expediting were the norm. Operating the routines of the purchasing team always took a back seat. When we examined the tasks and their impact on their cause and effect reality we developed some strategies to buy some time for the individual responsible for purchasing to shift their activities (from effect to cause). It only took a few weeks for noticeable results to emerge and the time 'bought' was paid back with interest.

Whether this lack of cause and effect thinking is down to personal preference, or a lack of having visibility of the bigger picture (if I do this - it affects the other team...) I don't know. What I do know is that if you review your business processes and define routines that support the tasks that are at cause, you can make a big shift in terms of how your business performs whilst eliminating unnecessary cape wearing.

Create your routine

The actual creating of a routine that can drive the right kinds of behaviours and ultimately form cape minimising habits is straightforward and follows these main steps:

- Review the outputs (effects) you need to achieve in your business.
- Determine the input activities (causes) required to stimulate the outputs.
- Decide on the frequency / timetable of the input activities.
- Agree who has responsibility for the input activities.
- Draw up / formalise the routine and publish it.
- Communicate and manage the execution of the routine.

One thing I should stress about the word 'routine' is that I am not referring to a crushing, minute-by-minute, calendar of events. I am guiding you towards a framework of activity that will include specific time-based activities. For example, if the routine requires a meeting about your customer orders at 3pm each day and there is nothing else defined for that day don't worry, the existing work activity is meant to fill the gap!

This routine should show the key, routine, repeating activities that when conducted eliminate the fire-fighting, cape wearing, reactive mode that we often find ourselves in. The routine should help you to boost productivity and improve how you deliver value for your customers. The art in creating your routine is to ensure that the input activities you define include 'checks and balances' to tie the rest of the working week together.

When I say 'checks and balances' I am referring to those yes / no discussions that will allow you to quickly manage the large chunks of time in-between the routine meetings that make up part of your schedule. As an example, one of my clients used to suffer from poor information being passed through their business. There were key elements within the required data that was expected to be compiled before being handed over. The simple routine meeting that we improved (they already had a daily meeting, we just augmented it) incorporated one additional question – "has all of the planning data been completed for today's launching projects?" The answer is either 'yes', or 'no'. There is no in-between answer. Obviously a 'yes' answer is what the team were aiming for. A 'no' answer led to the supplementary question "when will the data be ready?". Like all habits, this took a few days to become useful as a question because it took a little while to refocus the team's efforts and produce what needed to be produced, but thereafter it became both manageable and productive.

What I should point out here, from this example, is that the team who were not producing the data in a timely manner were producing the data at a later date in the delivery team's project; there were no extra demands in terms of the workload by introducing this question. The reality was that the planning data was produced late, under pressure, when the project was stalled as result of having no data. The planning team were (until this point) in a perpetual loop of not preparing the data, watching the project launch and fire-fighting the data at a critical point in the project... In this case, and many others I have seen, there is a short uncomfortable window where this situation needs to be rectified. The loop has to be broken in order to get back into a proper cause and effect relationship and this can take some management juggling of resources, expectations and activities in order to achieve.

If you find yourself in this quandary when you spot the back to front nature of your current routines (as opposed to your desired routines) then please don't ignore this challenge. When you get yourself out of the cape wearing loop and into pro-active management routines the performance of your team / division / business can really soar.

How do you measure your performance?

On top of the 'yes / no' questions that you can establish, there are two additional ways to measure the performance of your routines that I would like to touch on.

Appropriate measures are the first item. Do you have measures (also known as metrics or KPIs) that can help you figure out what the performance of your routine is? There is often a lag between receiving a series of 'yes' answers and the scores of your metrics improving, but it does give you another perspective. I'm not suggesting that your team may lie when answering the checks and balances questions, but it is helpful to have another viewpoint to help you become reassured as to the performance of your routine. If you don't have some KPIs that are currently suitable for this task don't worry, we will come back to this very topic later in this book.

The other item that I wanted to mention was defining some standards to manage against. We are all human and therefore prone to occasional failure. We also work in businesses that are dynamic (to say the least). If you decide that completing elements of your routine successfully four times out of five would be acceptable for your business then you have an expectation that can be managed. Five out of five (in this example) would be excellent, four out of five would be expected and three out of five (or less) needs attention. You can have standards elsewhere in your business too that can help you gain a perspective of whether your routine is being effective or not. If you recall the section on defining a utopian view of the future you can expand / incorporate those ideas into your day to day management activities. If you decide what effects you want to see in the business, as a result of having an effective routine, you can then go and look for them.

For example, if you have a routine that should improve how the workload is accepted into your business then you should be able to experience fewer customers grumbling about late orders. As another example, if you have built a routine to update team level management information on their departmental noticeboards each week then you should never see out of date information on the noticeboards. Defining standards is a great way to complement KPIs and routine 'checks and balances' meetings to give you a fuller picture as to what the performance of your routine is.

With your routine, checks and balances, KPIs and standards you now have a good platform to start monitoring your direction of travel. Direction of travel is a widely used term that allows us to work out if our businesses are heading in the right direction. Many businesses look at snapshots only, but put enough snapshots together and you have a story. Is the story heading upwards (to victory), heading downwards (to failure), or staying put (Groundhog Day!). Now, depending on where your starting position is, those three directions can make a huge difference to how you need to respond. If your business is committed to driving out the capes, you can use this information to guide your decisions, tactics and plans so that you can continue to push your business' performance in the right direction.

Formalising your routine reporting

Formality seems to be a divisive approach to business. I like, and value, being free to create solutions and ideas to help my clients. When I was employed I liked being given a free-reign to think and create, but I also respected the need for formality in a business. You can see a spectrum of formality in the business sector; some are loose and some are rigid. For me, finding the right balance is essential if you want to eliminate your capes. You need the flexibility and creativity to come up with new approaches and ideas that can boost your productivity and the ability to delight your customers. You need the rigidity of discipline and routine to make sure that the business churns out its products, services and projects in a robust and repeatable way (so that the goals of both you and your customer are met).

If you want to find your direction of travel you will need to define a formal reporting frequency, effectively an extension to your business routine.

When do you want to know what, from whom?

This is the simple question that needs to be answered. If this is relatively new to you I propose that you look at two horizons; what do you want to know each week and what do you want to know each month. Of course, you can change this to shorter and longer periods (down to hours and up to one year, for example). I don't want you to get bogged down with coming up with a formal reporting structure, I want you to quickly get some good information flowing to you that you can use to re-direct your teams so that your capes reduce and your overall performance increases. Once you have become comfortable with version '1.0' of your reporting structure you can then expand it to become the bigger and better version that it is destined to become (without becoming an administrative burden!).

To access a free reporting template, visit the downloads page via the Links chapter.

It might also be necessary for you to help define the reports that you will need – the headings, the type of content and where to circulate / submit the report to. I find that many initiatives of this nature fail because of an unclear expression of exactly what is wanted and this approach then falls over due to frustration on all sides (in a similar nature to the non-use of a PID on projects!). Again, don't get bogged down with the reporting templates, get something that is approximately right and improve the format with each successive submission. Everyone will be learning with this one! My final point on this item is don't get fazed by the first submission. If you haven't been in the swing of reporting on a regular basis (and have a lot of loose ends floating around the business) then the first report may be a little on the heavy side! Give the reporting two or three weeks to calm down before you start getting critical on the content.

Formal reviews

Having the reporting is a great step forward. Having the means to review, make sense and re-direct the activities is another issue altogether. Luckily, it is a relatively straightforward affair and needs only someone to pick a time slot on a regular basis to do just this (hey – isn't this a routine?).

Agree on how the review will take place. Will it be face to face, via email, or another technology that has been invented since the time this book has been written?

I prefer face to face and I know that plenty of my clients do too. It makes the review important, it makes it meaningful and it makes the act of decision making easier and quicker in many cases (but please take a time out to deliberate if required).

These formal reviews should allow you to find out if:
- the key tasks from your routine are being adhered to,
- the defined routines are effective,
- the requested standards are being made,
- the performance measures of the business are showing positive signs,
- the direction of travel is pointing the right way!

If you put all of the items from this chapter together you should have created a powerful management approach that can really help you to drive out the capes, the inefficiencies and ineffectiveness that lurks in your business. In summary, an effective routine can transform how your business works!

Action Points

- Create a routine that serves your business by identifying the actions / events / tasks that cause the effects that you want to experience. Include responsibilities also.
- Review your existing suite of business measures (Key Performance Indicators) and add in any additional 'input' or 'process' metrics that would help you to steer your business in the right direction.

- Decide if you need to implement a formal reporting approach, and if you do how it would operate.

Leading by Example

A huge factor in eliminating capes from your business is you.

Do you lead by example with the topics we have covered up to this point?

Do you provide clear direction to your teams?

Do you run the established reporting structures that your business needs?

Do you dig to the root cause of problems before trying to resolve issues?

How you behave and act each day, both in front of and away from your colleagues, has an impact on the behaviour of others. What you do has an influence on the number of capes that will need to be worn in the coming hours, days and months.

Are you at cause?

What I am getting at is this – are you operating primarily from a causal position?

Do you fly around in a 'flap' trying to put out fires yourself, or are you more of a cool, calm operator?

Of course, I don't mean 100% of the time because that is unrealistic for pretty much all of us. As I said at the start of this book there will be legitimate times to wear a cape and I would expect you to do what is required when the unforeseen occurs. But, what is your primary mode of operating? Are you mostly calm or are you mostly flapping?

Take stock of how your days play out. If you picked up this book because you felt you needed to, then I fear that there is a good chance that you are stuck in the 'at effect' category. For now, take stock of where you are and as you progress through the implementation of the ideas in this book monitor how your days start to fare.

What impact do you have on the use of the cape?

Related to how you spend your days is understanding what things you do (or don't do) that cause others to wear a cape. I was discussing the idea of wearing capes with one of my clients and they eventually made a statement that summarised this point:

"Are they the fire-fighter, or the arsonist?"

At the same time as we have to wear capes in our business we may also be creating situations that make others have to wear capes too. If you have worked through the exercises in this book already you may now have some idea as to what impact you may be having on both your own teams and the wider business.

Do you need to change also?

So, do you need to come up with a personal action plan for yourself?

If some of the improvements in your business are linked to your own personal behaviours then it will most likely be worthwhile to have a plan for yourself. Sharing your personal development actions with your colleagues might be a noble activity and declaring your intentions might be a common goal setting strategy, but it might detract the focus your team need to have with the business' core improvement plans. It may also be uncomfortable if you aren't making the progress you had hoped for.

A better alternative is to find an ally in the business that you can work with. Ideally this other person will want to iron out some of their own behaviours and also wish to see a reduction in cape wearing events. Essentially you would be making a pact together, but I'm going to leave this point here. I'm sure that this topic is a personal development book in its own right!

The handful of personal development areas that might be worth considering when it comes to banishing the capes from your business include:
- Setting clear objectives for your team.
- Developing effective routines.
- Being disciplined (in the sense of doing what you previously committed to doing).
- Setting and managing standards.
- Using KPIs effectively.
- Being skilful at using root cause problem solving techniques.
- Chairing punchy 'checks and balances' type meetings.

… and I am sure you can add a number of additional points that are buzzing round your head right now!

Take stock of your influence on the need for wearing capes, figure out if you are the cause of any capes and develop an action plan as required. In the next section I will share with you some of my ideas around coaching your key staff to help you lead your business to victory against the capes.

Action Points

- Review how you operate day to day and make sure that you are leading by example. If you have a few flaws to deal with, identify them and come up with a plan to ensure that you are an exemplar of what good looks like.
- Look at the additional development areas listed above and decide if you want to incorporate any of those areas into your personal development plan.

Coaching the Cape Away

When you reflect on the people in your business you will most likely realise that you have an imbalance in terms of the skills, habits and behaviours that you have present. Some people will want to make the workplace more productive, more effective and a better place to be. Some won't, or can't.

If you identify the people that want to actively join you during this period of change, you can direct some of your efforts to these individuals and effectively multiply the business' capacity for making change happen. By sharing the load, you can drive out the capes together, gather momentum faster and lead the others to a more productive working environment.

One on one time

Dedicating time to the handful of people you have identified might feel like a stretch if you feel overwhelmed already with your workload. What I want you to appreciate here is that, if you can devise a strategy to protect some of your precious time with someone else that fundamentally wants the same things as you, there is the potential to really accelerate the rate of change (more so than if it is just you on your own).

Just imagine having more than one of you identifying new improvement opportunities to eliminate unnecessary capes from your business. Would that be of interest? Would it be worth the very short-term inconvenience to make both of your lives easier and achieve the business' goals faster?

I mentioned a moment ago that, if you identify some

strategies, this is possible. What strategies do you have available to you? Could you:

- Ask a colleague to protect your diary/take your mobile phone so that you can dedicate some time to this?
- Cancel some meetings that are low(er) value to free up some time?
- Use the first half hour of the day to solely focus on this kind of work?
- Work on the same basis as if you were sick and not be in the business physically for a day (whilst you work on coaching your colleagues)?
- Speak to your boss and get some of your responsibilities temporarily covered by another colleague?

Do you think it might be possible to carve out some time from your hectic week to organise this? Many of my clients have realised that a lot of the working day is ineffective and therefore compressing the day slightly, or re-organising who does what, can allow for time to be freed up whilst still delivering the business' outputs.

Being a guide

Although this section of the book could never be a complete guide to coaching an individual, or your team, there are a few basic points that I would like to cover with you.

1. Show them how to get around the obstacle, don't carry them.

The most essential point is that you want this person (or, persons) to be more able to help you eliminate the capes from your business through the better application of process management and acting at cause. Sharing with them the ideas from this book is a good place to start and then you can work through the issues that are plaguing your business. However, when the person you are coaching gets stuck, you need to discuss with them what they are facing and ask them how they could go about getting past this obstacle. If you tell them exactly what to do they miss out on the learning experience and don't get better at the rate that you would like. Of course, if they are completely stuck, it is reasonable to give them a nudge. Getting the balance right in this kind of relationship (as opposed to a sub-ordinate relationship where you can just tell them what to do) can be difficult if you have never done it before. Remember the point is that you want these chosen individuals to develop their skills and you are to be a guide, not a manager, in this context.

2. Use the PID approach to help direct them.

Earlier I shared with you the use of Project Initiation Documents (PIDs) to help clarify what a specific improvement project is designed to do. In a coaching relationship, having a PID can help by specifying what is and isn't included in the project (as well as what is to be delivered!) and can really help to keep the person you are coaching on the straight and narrow.

The PID can be used as a reference point for their development and gives a simple starting point for any conversations you will have about both them and their project. It can be really easy to skip the creation of a PID when you start a new improvement activity, but the benefits of getting your project off on the right foot, and ending in the right way, massively outweigh the time and effort it takes to create a PID in the first place.

3. Keep talking.

The final point I want to make on this brief look into coaching your key players is that you need to keep talking. If you don't have a natural conversation as part of your working day I urge you to schedule some time to make sure that you do speak. A phone call, a ten minute catch up each day, an email round up each week, or whatever else that works for both of you. I often see a relationship form and then break down quickly due to people being busy (or at least perceived to be busy) and not realising the importance of this arrangement; the short-term rush is at the expense of the longer-term gain.

The payback from learning and deploying practical skills can be huge for a business. Don't get stuck in the busy-ness of normal working practices. It might feel pressured to take some time out each day to bring on your key staff, but once they are up and away you will have an increased capacity to deliver change and improvement within your business. Once you make some changes and you don't need to wear the cape so often then you will see a natural rise in available time to work in the business. You have a choice as to whether you want to go around in circles, or start to break free from the cape wearing cycle. Bear in mind that if it was easy to break free you would have done it already. Make the decision and consider using this coaching approach as a potential strategy to make a difference to your business.

An employee that I worked alongside during a project took on more and more work themselves, ultimately putting them in numerous cape situations. When it was clear that this scenario wasn't going to change anytime soon, I asked them about sharing out the workload with one of their colleagues. They replied that it would take too much time to train them and they could do it faster. I had gotten to know both of these people quite well during the project, so I challenged this comment. When the training time was taken into account, along with the fact that the other person's time was under-utilised, it made perfect sense to undertake the training and take the short-term hit. What made sense in the moment made no sense in the longer term. Beware of this trap.

Serving those who need it

Unfortunately, not all of your staff will be equal when it comes to helping you remove the unnecessary capes from your business. As I am sure that you are aware from your normal day to day activities, there are some of your team that will have a positive impact, and there are some that will have the opposite.

You have limited time. I understand that, so I propose that you split your time between these two groups so that:
- You spend the majority of your available coaching time with the few individuals that will truly help to implement the right kinds of behaviours and disciplines.
- You spend a small portion of your time with the 'unhelpers' to provide the right facts about what you are doing (solely so that you limit their effect on the other people in the business).

There are many schools of thought on how you should handle the negative folk in a business and I have still never found a right, or perfect, answer. During my time as a manager, and working with my clients, I have found the above to be effective. I'm sure that you don't need the following warning, but I'll give it anyway. Don't pander to the negative bunch, they will suck away your time and destroy your ability to be effective.

The penny can drop with the negative group and they can often move from a position of being negative to being neutral. But, if you are wasting your time with this bunch please feel free to move away from them!

You know your staff best, so please choose a coaching strategy that makes sense for your business.

Tying this in with the other approaches

You have probably figured out the links between this light approach to coaching and the other ideas in this book. When you have a small group around you all working towards the improvement of the business and the reduction of cape wearing episodes you will be able to:

- Link with your view of utopia and share with your team the vision you are working towards. This will help them gain clarity of what a world without capes could look like.
- Achieve KPI ownership by sharing out the accountability for performance. If each of your team have the ability to monitor, adapt and improve the performance of specific business processes, you will significantly improve the rate of change you experience.
- Improve the reporting your business experiences. If you can get to a point where useful information is being supplied on a regular basis then more of your decisions can be based on fact. I have no issue with gut feeling being used, but knowing the facts can provide

insights that you may miss otherwise and hopefully will support your gut feelings.

- Implement more change projects. More people means a greater ability to manage and deliver more change activity through your business. You still run the risk of overwhelming your business with change, but as a minimum you will have more brains dedicated to the quest for improvement, which you can then throttle as appropriate. This is certainly a stronger position than under resourcing this aspect of improvement; you can't throttle up if you don't have the resources available!

Make the elimination of capes a normal part of business life and talk about it regularly, especially with the core group that you are coaching. Engaging with your staff, sharing ideas, learning from each other and experimenting together are all strategies that can accelerate your progress.

I used to have a Team Leader report to me who was in pure firefighting mode for his entire working week. His week was miserable, he certainly didn't relish the need to wear a cape constantly. I tried to help him; each week was another wave of instruction and suggestions that I wanted him to execute. Nothing stuck, nothing took hold until the relationship changed. Instead of instruction I shared with him my vision for how the business unit could operate. I invited him to develop this view of the future and over a period of weeks we started to formalise our plans for what we wanted to achieve. We worked together on our plans; I shared with him tools and methods and he shared his ideas and practical knowledge with me.

The performance of his production department transformed over a three-month period. We used a KPI called OEE (Overall

Equipment Effectiveness) to track our performance. If you have used OEE before you will know that it is a composite KPI that multiplies your equipment availability by the rate of production by the quality of the output. Our OEE was bubbling around the 6% to 7% mark... World class is considered to be 85% OEE, and after our three-month focus we stabilised our OEE at around 80%. Day to day life was completely different. On time delivery was a breeze, quality was guaranteed and our frustrations just about eliminated.

If I hadn't worked with my Team Leader in a coaching relationship I don't think that we would have achieved the results that we experienced. My predecessor was a 'shout and command' kind of guy and I could see that this approach hadn't worked. The history of the business unit showed that my predecessor's predecessor hadn't figured it out either. But, and here is the real point, change doesn't take long when you have the right kind of relationship.

I accept that this section on coaching will seem light if you are a coaching professional yourself, I am not proposing the advice in this chapter as being a definitive guide to coaching. I am proposing, however, that as with many things in life, you can get a long way by doing a few of the right things. Find a few people that could help you improve your business, share your view of the future, help them to help themselves around their obstacles and keep a conversation running throughout the change period (and forever if you can!).

In the next section I am going to share with you some of my thoughts around creating decent action plans that you (and now your band of helpers) can use to establish change in your business even more effectively. The capes soon won't know what's hit them!

Action Points

-   Identify who on your team you want to invest time in to coach them in order to accelerate the removal of capes from the business.
-   Determine the best way to spend time with these individuals; one to one, or as a group.
-   Think through the types of obstacles that they will hit as they reach out on their own to help improve the business and prepare some guidance based responses so that you don't jump in to doing the work for them when the going gets tough.

Creating Your Own Action Plans

Little happens in many businesses without an accountable action plan, formal or informal. This is a fact of life. To eliminate capes from our businesses we need an idea of where the capes are, a view on the possible future, help from our team, solid project outlines and a good plan.

I see many plans as I travel from business to business and some are certainly better than others. This section of the book shares some practical ideas on setting up your actions plans and managing them. If you are the kind of personality that leans towards that of being a 'perfectionist' then please let me urge you to operate with speed and adopt a 'fit for purpose' stance. Improvement and speed go well together when the idea is good. I would personally prefer a scruffy looking plan that made sense and achieved results over a perfectly polished plan that doesn't get implemented.

Let's dive in!

Knowing where to start

Defining a clear outcome is the place to start. Being able to articulate what you want to experience at the end of the improvement is where you need to begin. Once you have a good outcome you can feed this into your PIDs, when you are ready to create them.

You know where you are today. But what if you are in a situation that is a real mess and you can't get your head lifted up long enough to draw out an objective that makes sense? A two-step plan would make a lot of sense in this case; step one is to deal with the immediate issues and then step two is to move towards a more optimal future situation, once you have had time to breathe and think about where you need to go. If you find yourself in this predicament, don't dismiss the idea of having a properly thought out action plan, just look at it as a two-stage process.

So, let's assume that you aren't in the middle of a crisis, how do you conjure your objective?

Remember the utopia document? This is a great place to start when defining the objective for your action plan. I should mention here that I said objective and plan. You can have as many plans as you want, but I recommend that you only have one objective per plan so that you can keep your planning as simple as possible.

Articulating your objective can be a struggle for some. If you have already drafted your utopia document as you read this book then you may have some empathy for those of us who struggle to capture our thoughts in writing. An approach that we have discussed elsewhere already is also available to help us with this challenge too; 5W1H.

If you recall this series of six questions from the root cause analysis chapter you will remember the sequence of who, what, where, when, why and how. If you use these words as prompts to shape your thoughts it should help you to capture something meaningful to help you communicate your objectives with your team and colleagues. I must point out that, in this particular application of 5W1H, the 'why?' prompt is less useful than when it was used with the 'five why' method and I don't want you to get hung up on trying to use it in this application.

If you can get across who will be doing what, where and how they will do it and when this takes place, you should be well placed to craft some excellent objectives.

Planning out the sequence

One interesting feature that I see when I review improvement plans is the 'and magic happens' part in the middle of the plan. Of course, I am joking, but it would make more sense if it was included in some of the plans I have seen! Let me express this differently; I see plenty of plans that have a clear starting point and initial actions. They often have a reasonable end to the plan (although agreeing on what the end of the plan is can be a challenge – see more in a moment). It's the bit in the middle that can be interesting. There is often a jump from the actions at the start (the obvious things that need to be done first) to the conclusion of the project. When I see my clients' staff undertaking projects like this, they often find that they make a promising start and then get lost. Their plan doesn't help them to reach the desired objective because the steps they need to follow are missing.

Of course, this isn't the case all of the time, but I would like to arm you with an approach that can help you create action plans that have all of the steps present. The backwards planning method (otherwise known as the 'B to A method') is one of the best tools I have come across in my travels (unless you have access to someone who has already travelled the path you want to take and they are willing and able to share the information with you!).

To plan using the backwards planning method, you start at the end point (your objective) and imagine your way back to where you are today. This imagination exercise allows you to create a path which can form the improvement plan you are looking to undertake. Many people I work with reverse the backwards sequence and check to see if it still makes sense, and add in any additional steps that become obvious when put into the right order. Backwards planning might take a bit of practice to make it work for your business, but it is certainly a technique that can help you to quickly produce improvement plans once you have gotten a bit of experience under your belt.

Imagine that you are wanting to implement a self-service process into your business. In backwards planning, you may see yourself with the completed process in place and working well. You then ask yourself this question - 'what's the last thing that I would have done...?' and you repeat this question for each answer you get, until you reach your present position.

For example:
- The self-service process is working as it should (objective).
(What's the last thing that I / we would have done?)*
- I would have trained the team in the new process until they were competent.
- I would have ensured the new process was tested and working properly.
- I would have uploaded all of the documents to the cloud storage area.
- My team would have completed all of the forms required for the process.
- I would have specified the documents required for this project.
- We would have agreed on a solution to implement the new process.
- We would have mapped out a revised process.
- We would have listed all of the problems with the current process, and the opportunities for improvement.

- I would have arranged a team meeting to review the current process and the documentation it requires.
- I am back at the start!

* This question repeats between each example statement.

A final question that I would like to pose to you as you think about the end-point of your projects (aka, your real objective) is 'what is the real end point?' Is the end of your project when you switch on the machine / deploy the software / initiate the new process? Or, is it tied up somewhere after the standard operating procedures (SOPs) have been written, the training handbooks written, the training delivered, the coaching having been completed, the commissioning finished, or something else. It is a really disappointing aspect of continuous improvement to see a great project get through the final stage and then fall over because someone has forgotten all of the steps required at the end of the project. This becomes a continuous improvement cape wearing moment! Specify the final steps of your improvement plan with care...

To PID, or not to PID?

In a previous chapter I shared with you how to complete a PID (Project Initiation Document). PIDs are fantastic methods to communicate the boundaries and deliverables of a project, but do you need one in every situation?

As a manager it is up to you to decide if you want, or need, one for the project you are considering. For many businesses a threshold of project size, or complexity, is used to determine if a PID should be created, or not. This leaves us with three main options:
1 – Don't use PIDs at all.

2 – Use PIDs for projects of a certain size / complexity / duration.

3 – Use PIDs for every project.

If you choose not to use PIDs, or only in specific situation then please ensure that you have clarity of all of the features required. I find that PIDs and action plans go hand in hand and I am sure that you will find your own 'groove' when it comes to this.

The essentials of your action plan

Now that you have clarity on the actions for your action plan we can again revisit 5W1H to embellish the action steps. For each action step we can also articulate:

- Who is responsible for each action.
- When it needs to be completed by.
- What the specific outcome (or deliverable) of each action needs to be.
- How the task is to be completed (if guidance is required).
- What the status of the task is (completed, in progress, on hold etc…).

Too many action plans do not include enough detail, or clues, as to what is required. Spending a little extra time to get the details confirmed can increase the chances of success when it comes to implementing the plan. Please invest this time, I assure you that it will be well worth the effort.

The format of the plan is up to you. If you use the description of the action and the above points as headings you should have a pretty good format to go with. If you are using standard office software then a spreadsheet will work well for creating a plan, especially if you can apply a filter to the status column so that you can focus on the tasks that are still to be completed (which works really well if you have lots of tasks on your action plan).

Once you have your action plan and you are able to publish it, I recommend that you hang it on a wall in a place where you and your team regularly work or meet. Making the plans visible is key to getting progress to be a reality. Plans that are hidden away on computers, or in desk drawers, don't get looked at as often and consequently don't get actioned (or even managed) as frequently. You're reading this book because you want to see some different results in your business, so make sure that your plans are highly visible. This approach will certainly help to keep the plans in people's minds and potentially accelerate the rate of delivery.

To access a free action plan template, to get your visible plans started, visit the downloads page via the Links chapter.

Short term, medium term and longer term

Creating improvement action plans can cause confusion for many of us.

How many plans are enough?

Do I need to have to one overall plan?

How do I coordinate between plans?

As you start to plan out your projects you may find that actions from one plan will provide inputs to other plans. I wouldn't worry about this too much. The aim of the game is to put in place positive improvements so that the need to wear our superhero cape reduces. I would much rather see twenty mini project plans that are being actioned than one mega plan that is 'perfect' and isn't getting followed.

So, don't get hung up on having one mega plan and instead focus on prioritising and coordinating your plans. Let me ask you some quick questions:
-   What improvements do you need to make today?
-   What improvements do you need to complete this month?
-   What improvements do you need to have in place within the next six months?

Answering these questions will help you to define a relative priority for your activities. I discussed earlier that not all improvements are equal when it comes to delivering results and you should bear this in mind when you decide what you need to focus on.

How fast can you go?

A point I should mention here is that your ability to deliver change, on top of your current day job, will be limited. No one can spend more than twenty-four hours a day on a project, so there is a natural ceiling that we all have to contend with. Assuming that you have a more typical working pattern of about forty hours per week, your improvement time will be somewhat less than that.

This is an important consideration to make when pulling together your action plans as the deadlines you define for each of your action tasks will most likely be either:
1.   An imposed deadline by another party.

2. Determined by how quickly you think you can get around to completing the task.

Imposed deadlines are a little out of your control (but you could always try to negotiate!) and need to be managed around your other tasks. The deadlines that you define are something that you can figure out and I suggest that the following points are taken into consideration:
- Find out how much time you think you have per week to focus on improvement activity.
- Halve this time, so that it is more realistic.
- Estimate how much time each task will take.
- Schedule the tasks based on the work content of each task slotted into your throttled back available improvement time per week.

This is a rough formula to help you schedule your improvement plans, but a good starting point if you are new to this.

Tie into the regular reporting structure

One strategy that is really effective in managing your improvement plans is to tie them into your regular reporting structure. If you have a regular management forum to discuss improvement activity, then providing a status of your project(s) at that meeting makes good sense. As discussed earlier, tying your improvement activity into the existing routines of your business is a great way to get momentum on your progress.

If you don't have a meeting that you think that you could tie this to, and your business has enough discipline to introduce an additional reporting activity then feel free to create a new one, just for your improvement projects. This might feel like a big ask, but the level of reporting required to keep projects moving forward can be quite minimal. A good example of this is using a one side of A4 paper format to capture 'what happened this week' that can be discussed with a line manager. So, if you are going to ask your team heads for information about what has progressed during the last seven days with regards to the improvement projects, you may only get a sentence or two on each project. It doesn't take long to write and it doesn't take long to read. Of course, there will be someone in your team who will try to write a page on each project. Don't let them, make it clear to them that this type of reporting is designed to be brief. The idea is to keep information flowing, to not create another time-consuming task for the individuals involved.

Another strategy is to have a projects board in one of your offices and create a short meeting that revolves around the board. At this meeting you can quickly run through the actions that have been completed and obstacles that need addressing since the last meeting. Even with a number of projects running simultaneously, you can run through a meeting like this in under ten minutes, as long as everyone is disciplined to keep their actions updated and keep the discussion focussed on the projects at hand.

However you think the reviewing of your projects would work best for your business, I recommend that the option you take blends speed and focus so that it is an easy thing for your teams to engage with. Short and pointed reviews allow the manager to respond to the updates and for the participants to react to the feedback. If the process of providing feedback is slow and sluggish it can become a chore. It shouldn't be, it should be a fun and interesting and a personal development opportunity. Good feedback and rapid responses can lead to dramatic and quick changes that can positively improve the performance of a business and help us to wave goodbye to the capes we once used to wear.

A common criticism when putting in place a feedback process like any of the ones I have suggested above is that people are already struggling for time. From a face-value perspective this would appear to be entirely true. However, there is an opportunity to challenge this thinking, as it is most likely to be the same thinking that forces us down a path of having to live with the firefighting that happens right now. If you get this criticism (or if you are feeling this way too) then counter it with the logic that if you create some time (it is possible) to make the changes happen, then you should then experience even more time being freed up later on as your improvements take effect. I pushed this to a logical conclusion in one of my jobs (as a Production Manager) where I got rid of so much no / low value activity that I was eventually able to eliminate my own job! I'm not suggesting for a minute that you should strive to do the same, but there might be elements of your job that you might want to consider this for. As I write this section of the book I am helping one business to eliminate 85% of the administrative content of one of their business processes. We're doing this because of a lack of available staff capable of doing the task and the fact that, when you look at the task, it is a bottleneck in the business and getting rid of most of it will help to improve customer satisfaction levels. So, if you think that you don't have time to have these kinds of reviews, it is probably more of a case that you can't afford not to make time to have them. After the first couple of weeks (struggling to fit the improvement tasks and their reviews into your working week) it should start to relax and you will be able to gain momentum thereafter. Of course, it does mean that you must choose some effective improvement actions to undertake in the first place!

At this point in the book you should have a fairly good idea of how to spot cape wearing moments in your business and have an idea about how you're going to take your business past the world of capes. Before I look at the world after the (unnecessary) capes, let me talk for a moment about getting excited about change…

Action Points

-   Try out the 'B to A' method and see if you can put it to good use.
-   Ensure that you don't create plans that have missing steps.
-   Download the action plan template and then tailor it to suit your business' needs.
-   Establish how much time you have per week to dedicate to improvement projects and make sure it is realistic (not optimistic).
-   Decide what regular reporting / review method would work best for your business, what frequency it would need to be carried out and by whom.

Becoming an Evangelist

Changing behaviours is difficult and could be the topic of an entire book. If you want your team to start working in a way that eliminates the need for cape-wearing, you need to find ways to help them change their behaviours.

I have already talked you through articulating a better vision of the future (through the utopia approach), tying your aspirations to reduce the need for cape wearing into your business routines and creating focused projects to help get the message across.

As I write this I am assuming that you are leading by example, but are you doing it with enthusiasm? Being evangelical about a facet of your business that you are trying to change is another strategy that you can employ to infect others with your enthusiasm to encourage them to engage with the changes that you need to make happen.

What is your focus?

Picking a primary focus for your enthusiastic energies is the first port of call. It is unlikely that you will have the time, or energy, to get really enthusiastic and fly the flag for more than one topic at a time on top of your day job. I recall a period of time at one of my clients where the whole management team got excited about a change that needed to happen. Like a Mexican wave, the messages and support flowed through the business. The change was completed in a couple of months (the problem had persisted for the previous five years and the capes were always on standby). If you looked past the management team however, you could find one director who was the nucleus of the excitement.

This one director talked constantly about the improvement. They spoke about the benefits at every opportunity and they weren't boring or flogging a dead horse, they just needed time for the other managers of the business to become infected with the idea that the future could be different.

In one of my previous roles I got excited about the quality and quantity of feedback that the production teams provided to me. They initially thought I was mad to want this kind of information; previous managers had not wanted a true two-way relationship with their staff. I kept on giving them opportunities to debate ideas, to share new opportunities that I had not seen and to provide a level of clarity between myself and themselves that had been lacking up until that point. Our 35% on time delivery performance soared to over 95% (rolling average) in just a few months. During that same period the department moved from loss making into profit, and the profitability increased month on month. It was a success for all of us, not just myself as a manager. One painful-to-operate machine that strained to produce thirty items in a shift easily romped past the eighty per shift mark, all because the operators were willing (through initial encouragement) to ask questions and explore their ideas.

If you had to get excited about one topic, to make it the primary focus for your cape reduction exercises, what would it be?

Can you get excited about it?

In the examples above there was a level of excitement present.

The capes had to go and there was someone who was excited about the idea of them going who could get others excited about it too!

Hopefully you can think of lots and lots of reasons why it would be good for everyone to get onboard with the improvement you have chosen to focus on. More importantly, the improvement should have a direct benefit to yourself and provide the drive required to make you talk about it all the time and allow you to become infectious with your enthusiasm.

A long time ago I worked with a very nice gentleman who, despite being keen to come across as wanting to change his part of the business for the better, seemed to oppose every improvement opportunity that came his way. Topics for discussion about improvement were shot down before they got started and I was feeling a little confused as to this person's intentions. Eventually this relationship came to a head and I asked him why he wanted to make these changes for the business. His response was a rote reply about the growth plans for the business and the need to execute strategy. Great answers, but not what I wanted. I pushed him again about why he was willing to make the changes, asking again what was in it for him.

He paused and looked out the window. As he moved his head I could see a collection of photo frames, each frame featuring his daughters dressed up as cute fairies and princesses. I asked him about his daughters and then challenged him to come up with a better answer. A couple of moments later he shook his head and then told me how little time he got to spend with his family (and another child was on the way!) due to the poor methods of working currently employed. Sure, he was the factory's hero, working each evening and most weekends to fix all of the production schedules, but this came at a cost - one that he was no longer willing to pay.

We talked about cause and effect and reviewed the improvement opportunities that he had shot down to date. After a few minutes of this review a clear pattern started to emerge about why he had to work the way he had to work. A clear path forward emerged and my newly motivated friend had a brilliant reason to push the improvement and make it happen. He got excited about the proper loading of sales orders into regional areas. This might be the most boring topic in the world to another person, but in this context, it had meaning, opportunity and a better lifestyle all wrapped together. The results of that piece of work were actually quite staggering when I consider the initial view of the potential for the change. A twenty-hour administrative process dropped to four hours and then eventually disappeared thanks to the efforts of this person, and the knock-on effects for both the business and his personal life were greatly appreciated by those affected.

This person had a brilliant 'why' for them to get excited by, which in turn made them evangelical about the subject for the improvement. This style of activity brought the others onboard and provided the energy to see the improvements through.

If you are reading this and wondering if you can get as excited as this, take a few minutes out from this book and see how many reasons you can come up with for why your chosen topic is important. As with the example above, come up with both personal and business reasons. If you don't find yourself getting excited then either look harder for better reasons to do it, or look for another topic that you can get excited by.

One factory, one schedule

To help you share your vision, try to package your evangelistic energy into a simple mantra. This will make your ongoing reinforcement of your focus much easier. A good example of this is the 'one factory, one schedule' phrase that I drilled into everyone at a factory I used to manage (until they saw the results that is!). In this particular case, our superhero character was an expediter and they came to the rescue by taking the customer's complaints and navigating their production orders through the business in the shortest period of time possible. The problem with this cape wearing approach was that the disruption it caused took the business to a worse place than where it originally was.

To make matters worse this person's role was not meant to be an expediter, but a scheduler! Their job was to schedule the work through the factory; effectively their interventions contravened what they were there to do in the first place.

When I took over the role of the Operations Manager I was soon inundated with calls from customers that were unhappy with our ever-slipping delivery schedules. My observations about the disruption caused by the continuous re-jiggling of production schedules was not welcomed and led to a lot of friction amongst the team (it's what they had always done) and it ended with the superhero of our story deciding to leave the business. Naturally my boss' instinct was to lump the expediting /scheduling activity onto my role and see what happened. I didn't want this poor level of performance on my CV, so I looked at what decisions were sitting behind these issues and found out that there were only a handful of things I had to change (there were actually sixteen things, but I'm just going to focus on the big hitters here). The top three changes were:

1. Sorting out the capacity plan and the rules for loading the business.
2. Allowing the factory's schedule to be driven by the capacity plan.
3. Helping the Team Leaders to do what the Team Leaders were meant to do.

And, as you know already, this led to the phrase 'one factory, one schedule'. One of the side effects of chopping and changing production through the business was that the lead times for production became bloated through a combination of inefficiency and ineffectiveness. There was no flow to production. Our production lead time had actually risen to over 18 weeks and when you consider the actual work content was just under three weeks (the product lived in a tank for nearly two weeks), this was quite some expansion of the original time frame.

At every meeting I went to where there was some kind of issue with production, customer satisfaction levels, planned maintenance or even just general management meetings, I would find myself re-stating the objective of 'one factory, one schedule'. To support my message, I captured and reported two key metrics; our OTIF (On Time In Full) performance level and our production lead time. As life started to become simpler through our customers not grumbling quite so much people could see our key metrics starting to improve. A correlation was starting to form and more people got behind the 'one factory, one schedule' mantra. Over a three-month period, our OTIF levels rose from the low 20s to over 98% average and our lead time came down to around three and a half weeks. Life was a lot more controlled and calmer on a day to day basis. Our capes were hung up to be saved for real emergencies.

Oh, and one of the real benefits was that we became known as one of the best performers in our sector and watched as our turnover tripled with no extra staff and our profitability went through the roof as we better utilised our existing resources.

Can you think of a mantra that would help your business focus on one of your key improvement areas?

As I write this I have just finished working with a client that had a problem with part of their material control function. There were a number of activities that needed to happen, but one of their key activities was the booking in of goods through their stores. Their mantra was 'no label – no move', referring to the fact that a pallet cannot be transferred into the business until a batch label is applied to the pallet itself. A very simple phrase, but one that was easily repeated amongst the staff every time there was a pallet space dilemma or a stock accuracy issue. The team soon got the message and started to behave in the right way.

Another business that had been struggling with the juggling of their day to day customer demands realised that behind all of the seemingly chaotic activity was a very structured process. This process needed key inputs at key times and, when you peeled away the frenetic action, it was theoretically a simple series of steps that needed to be managed (what isn't?). They developed a routine to support that process and agreed that the 'routine is everything'. When someone didn't have time to undertake a task – the 'routine is everything' was reminded to them. It worked and guess what? Their performance increased, their need to wear their superhero capes diminished and the limited spare time that they found in their days was re-directed into continuous improvement activities which further improved their customer's experience, allowed them to expand within their existing capacity and made the staff's days far more enjoyable.

So, have you thought up a phrase or mantra to summarise what you need your colleagues to focus on when the going gets a little tough?

I recommend that you put some thought into this so when you find yourself in a conversation about why something is going awry you can trot out your phrase. It might feel a little cheesy the first time around, but after a couple of times used it will start to have impact. Like most memes the phrase might be short, but the information that it conveys can be quite extensive. Going back to the 'one factory, one schedule' statement, this implies quite a lot. It implies that our contract review process is working correctly. It implies that the sales team have bought into the demand management requirements of both the customers and the factory. It implies that the purchasing function is aligned with the customer order book. It implies that the engineering function is able to support production.

One statement can send a very strong message.

Keep talking about it

This should go without saying! If you are being evangelical then you won't have a problem mentioning your number one focus at every opportunity. The aim of doing this is to sear it into your colleagues' minds, so that the value and importance of making this improvement is clear.

As mentioned earlier, if you have enough reasons why everyone should focus on your hot topic and there is enough pain in the business to make people want to change the current situation, then talking about this on an ongoing basis will not be a challenge. It might help you to have some prompts in the early days; meeting agenda points, memos on noticeboards, regular diary items – whatever it takes to form the habit of having this item in the front of everyone's minds.

Repetition is vital to ensuring that everyone else in your team understands the importance of what you are trying to focus on and it is your responsibility (if you are the evangelical one) to keep this repetition, this momentum, going.

Leading is about going first

On many occasions throughout my career people have debated with me the difference between management and leadership. Although this could again be a book in its own right, there is a simple summary that I would like to share with you. For me, management is about the management of processes and the rigour of activity. Leadership, by my definition, is about setting the direction and going first.

In many businesses that are stuck, no-one steps forward. This makes leadership even more important. If you are leading an improvement you will need to be seen at the front of the change activity. That includes being confused, getting it wrong, changing tack and risking being corrected by others. It doesn't matter in the long run, because it is the results that count.

This slight shift in approach, going first, can make a massive difference. Perhaps in the future there will be more people willing to take a lead when it comes to improvement activity, but for now it will have to be down to you. Go first and expect to be befuddled! Ironically, the cape wearers in our businesses don't seem to have the same level of self-consciousness about these sorts of things; they put on their capes and they leap straight into the spotlight…

Having enough reasons

I've already mentioned the need for having reasons. Having a strong enough 'why' behind a change is key to giving a strong enough story to get your staff to buy into. If you really want to put some 'oomph' into it from your perspective then have a look at making the change personal.

What would the change do for you, personally? What benefits would there be for you if you could see the change through? Will there be professional, financial or emotional gains to be had? What gets you fired up and can you get these kinds of results from seeing this change through?

If you can find enough personal answers to these questions then you will most likely find a level of motivation that will carry you through to the completion of the task and help you maintain your evangelical proclamations about the need for change. A gentleman who worked for me many years ago was fed up with a facet of his department that caused him bother on an ongoing basis. The problem was business wide and, although we had discussed possible solutions, nothing tangible was happening. Without any intention on my part I asked him 'why he didn't want to be known as the person who fixed this problem?' He didn't answer me immediately, but something must have been planted into his mind as the next day he seemed excited about the idea of being involved with finally putting this problem to bed, once and for all. I joked with him about him being the saviour of the business and even gave him a nickname. It was only after the change had been made, and he truly was the saviour, that I realised that the nickname allowed us to talk about the change on an ongoing basis so easily.

If you are wondering what the nickname was it was 'Mr TPM' (as in Total Productive Maintenance). Machines kept on breaking down (requiring cape wearing engineers and maintenance staff) and the subject with the operators seemed prickly. Mr TPM helped us to build a bridge between the operators and the maintenance staff whilst establishing the early version of our TPM system.

Making change a personal endeavour really can give you the motivation you need to see it through.

Hit it until you hit it

Persistence is required with change, and moving away from wearing capes by being evangelical about the changes that you have planned out will be no different. It will go wrong. It is likely that your best thought out plans will not always deliver the results you expected and they won't make the progress you had hoped for the first time around. Having said that, you might hit it lucky and be able to make some changes in your business and do it without having to deviate from your original plan. If this happens celebrate!

For the rest of us, the path will be windy and you will need to remember that, just because it is taking longer and / or is more difficult to get to your desired destination, you must not stop shouting from the rooftops about the change that needs to be made. When I was trying the get a shop floor booking system working in one of my previous roles I had to grit my teeth when it was going a little pear shaped and stick to my message of the change being worthwhile in the end. I knew that we were doing the right things and we just had to ride out some of the computer issues that we were facing. My clients have had to do the same thing too, when their improvements weren't going the right way and it was easy for people to throw their (metaphorical) rocks, we all kept going with the right messages. The messages are based on ideals and principles and they can never be wrong unless we give up.

Giving up is not an option.

If you keep on talking about what needs to happen, and keep on taking action to bring the change to life, you give yourself the best chance of getting there. Very few of my past successes, or my clients have been one-hit wonders. There has been iteration over the days, weeks and months to get the result required. Change might be simple, but it isn't always easy!

When you are battling against staff for whom wearing capes is all they know, the change process will need to be given time. Effectively you are reconditioning your team to think and behave in a different way. Having reasons for changing help, but it will most likely take repetition and persistence until they put two and two together and a light bulb moment happens. It might take days, it might take months, but as more and more people convert to a better way of working day-to-day, they too will start to perform the right kinds of activities if they want to join in with the growth and improvement plans of the business. The subject of what to do if they refuse to join the non-cape wearing team is a topic for your HR department!

I remember one Operations Manager who was struggling with a big overdue order book. We had agreed upon a few key changes as to how the business processes were going to be conducted and tried to implement them, but one in particular was not happening. Several months later, whilst other improvements had been made elsewhere, he looked up from his desk whilst we were having a meeting and re-stated our evangelical mantra ('every job is to start on time') in a way that made sense to him. The penny had dropped and the very next day his behaviours changed and this person was never the same again; productivity rose, effectiveness of the business rose and the overdue orders were ejected from the business at lighting pace. We could have written him off, but thankfully we didn't and he got there at his own pace. It was worth the wait too, the accomplishments this person made thereafter were brilliant, the overall performance and profitability of the business went from strength to strength. His mantra was 'every kit leaves the stores on time', a minor twist on our original statement, but one that clicked for him. Simple, yet powerful.

Transition time

And that's how it can happen. One day you seem to be struggling with the performance of your business as you keep on extolling the benefits of the changes that you need to make and then, suddenly, you realise that the business has changed and the superhero cape is being brought out less often.

It is not always obvious that the change is taking effect if you are busy with your day job. Small signs of improvement may get missed, but after a while you will start to see the improvements come. If you have been talking to the right people, in the right way, about the right things, you will have the best chance of making the change happen.

You might have noticed that I keep on talking about giving yourself the best chance of making the change happen. I can't guarantee you any results from this, or any other approach in this book. All I can do is share with you the best information I have at my disposal as I write. In my experience though, positive changes are possible and you should be able to transition from a chaotic working environment to an organised and efficient business that operates and plans from cause. What I can't promise is that you have the ability to deliver this, or that you will have the stamina to see the changes through… but you can make this promise to yourself, if you are ready to.

Now that you have started to plan your way out of cape-dom, I will share with you in the next chapter my thoughts on keeping your good work in place.

Action Points

- Pick a focus to become evangelical about, something that would really make a difference (or a positive statement if this is in your early days).
- Establish the reasons for both you and the business as to why this focus is worth getting excited about.
- Get excited and keep on talking about the improvement focus.
- Create a mantra, if it is appropriate. This is a slogan that is easy to remember and helps to embody all of the behaviours required to make the change happen.
- Lead from the front and keep going until you have achieved your victory.

Monitoring the Health of Your Processes

Now that you have moved into a working situation that requires fewer cape wearing superheroes, the question is this:

> "How do I make sure that we don't slip back into previous bad habits?"

It is a great question, and the right one for where you are now on this journey.

Getting past the immediate fix

On many occasions I have seen businesses make adjustments and get 'pumped up' from making these changes, only to slip back in a few weeks to their starting position. The truth is that working in a cape-less environment means working and behaving in a different way. This may seem obvious, and logical, but I need to stress it at this point because of the potential feral natures of your staff members. I referred to people having a natural feral state earlier on in this book and it really is an important factor to consider, enough for me to recap it here.

When you have a put a change into your business and the going gets tough, the new way of operating has to feel comfortable and be easy to do, otherwise it will lose out to the natural inclinations of the people that are under pressure. Steps will be missed, corners will be cut and, within hours, the need for people to wear capes will re-emerge. You will have capes flying everywhere if you don't watch out!

The following pointers will help you to avoid slipping back to your previous state.

Process driven KPIs

I have already touched on having Key Performance Indicators for your business. Having process driven KPIs will allow you to steer the activities and habits of the business so that you get the kinds of results that you want to experience. The 'yes / no' questions I referred to earlier in this book should be your starting point for reviewing the spread of measures you can actively use to keep your activities on track.

Remember, they are called 'key' for a reason; if you have too many they stop becoming meaningful. As a side note here, I have worked with a few organisations that had hundreds of measures and did not determine which ones were the key indicators. Meetings were jumbled and confused affairs – it was unclear what the immediate team should focus on. When we assigned the KPIs to different areas of the business and agreed on what was key at which level, they started to make sense in terms of how the business could use them to make day-to-day decisions.

But, if you still haven't created a suite of measures to serve your business let me give you a few pointers here:
- Look at the key steps in your business processes and identify where you can capture data about the performance of those steps.

- Get a balance between measures that reflect the activity at the input of the process, the middle of the process and the output.
- Many businesses have a tendency to look only at output metrics, which may well tell you a story, but they won't help you to change the outcome. Input and mid-way process measures can, however.
- Define what good looks like and set some targets / standards around each measure.
- Tie your measures into your meetings.
- Periodically increase your targets, in line with the increase in performance your business is experiencing.

The right selection and spread of measures can make a dramatic difference to the results your business achieves. Getting the right measures at the start and the middle of your processes can allow you to reinforce the right kinds of behaviours and remove the need to wear capes.

Regular, routine, meetings

Probably the strongest option you have for keeping the capes at bay and running your business operations in the way that they are designed is through good old-fashioned management. Remember the distinction I made between leadership and management in an earlier section? The leadership component largely comes to the fore when you are engaging with your teams and identifying the kinds of change that you want to experience. Management, on the other hand, comes to the fore when you need to execute the revised business processes and habits with high levels of effectiveness and efficiency. This is the time for good management.

Execution. It is a great word, isn't it? I talk with my clients about execution a lot. The reason for this is that once a business has gotten past the 'fun' of designing and experimenting with its processes it then moves over to the day-to-day running of the processes. Or, put another way, the business moves into a phase of executing its processes. When I am discussing with a business why things are going wrong, I often find myself having to restrain the leaders of the business from trying to invent a new solution when the answer is 'better execution'. For many people, executing the day to day activities isn't anywhere as near as exciting as designing and developing processes, and this is when your encouragement (and, again, leadership) will be needed to help settle your team down to make sure they move into their management roles.

Management includes making sure that the execution of the agreed tasks has taken place satisfactorily. It also means that agreed standards are respected and lived up to. Management thrives on routines and that is exactly what you should strive for as you aim for the fewest cape incidents possible by running and managing your business processes effectively.

Management meetings are a vehicle that every business can take advantage of to help keep their routines in place. I'm not talking about long, boring, stuffy and pointless meetings. I am talking about regular, short, punchy and meaningful meetings. Meetings that have clear actions. Meetings that have clear accountability. Meetings that make a difference and that your staff will see value in and want to participate in. For every key activity in your business you can identify a few 'killer questions' that will help everyone at the meeting determine as to whether the right kinds of habits are in place, based on the business' ability to deliver the right results without excessive headless-chicken type activities!

You don't need to have extensive meetings covering the entire working day. I am talking more along the lines of a few meetings that operate frequently throughout the course of the working week. Each business is different, but a few generic meeting types that can really help businesses to manage and monitor their activities include:

- Daily team 'huddles' to make sure that all of the key tasks (at cause) from the previous day have been completed successfully, the results (the effects) are where they should be and that any immediate actions are known to the group and the responsibility for their closure agreed.
- Capacity reviews to ensure that the business has the right kind of resource and right levels of resource in its different functions across the business.
- Senior Management reviews to ensure that all of the major business processes are functioning correctly and that any high-level business issues are being dealt with, as well as ensuring that the major inputs (sales, ideas, cash etc...) and outputs (services/products, profits, client experience etc...) are where they should be.
- Specific project reviews, pulling the key staff around specific projects to ensure that their delivery is as efficient and effective as possible, for the duration of the project.
- Sales and Operations Planning (S&OP) type meetings to balance out the demands of the customers, with the resources of the business, to achieve the business plan (and adjusting activity levels, resources, goals and timelines as required).

The purpose of each meeting is to have a regular, face to face, contact point where your KPIs and your 'killer questions' can be asked and answered. Obviously, the focus of each meeting and who you invite to those meetings will decide which questions and KPIs are appropriate for each meeting, the trick is to plan the meetings so that all of your KPIs and questions are utilised properly.

Building the structure for cape-less living

Right at the start of this book I mentioned that if resources are stretched then the number of instances of cape wearing that takes place might well be high. I am a fan of setting targets and then working towards those targets, including how many people it takes to handle a specific workload. This approach fosters the need for continuous improvement and it certainly provides the focus often needed to ensure that organisations aren't overstaffed.

However, there is the reality that the rate of improvement and the ability to eliminate the wasteful aspects of a person's role is limited. This means that getting the right staffing levels, perhaps through a mathematical approach to calculating work volumes and factoring in the distractions that take place in your business (also known as losses), needs to take place if you don't want to 'artificially' trigger cape episodes. I won't go any further into this topic, but let me finish this remark by saying that capacity planning isn't just for machines and production environments. Professional staff are similarly bound by their availability and share many of the same management requirements, so let's not forget this when reviewing the staffing levels of a business.

The other point I want to make about the structure of a business, when designing it for cape-less living (as in fewer capes, not zero – unfortunately), is the reporting structure. During most of my employed career I never got too excited about organisational structures. In most cases I had no say over who reported to me and who I reported to. As time progressed and I finally got a say in how these affairs worked, I eventually appreciated the importance of having the right people linked together. The roles, the personalities, the agendas, the needs, the objectives… they all make a difference in terms of how the structure could be formed. Again, this could be a topic for a whole other book, but there is one key point that I want to draw your attention to, one that can be practical in terms of how you apply the ideas in this book.

To live in a cape-less world there needs to be a certain degree of discipline. I am not specifically referring to written warnings, dismissals and the like, I am talking about doing what has been agreed, when it has been agreed. The problem areas of the business could benefit from having senior managers that have a lust for routine and discipline. Everyone is different and it is a fact of life that some people are more inclined towards regimentation and order. You could argue that the dictates of the business must be adhered to and so what I am offering here is a two-pronged approach to helping your business' structure support your goal of a less chaotic, more controlled and cape-less workplace.

Just last week I was in a conversation with a senior manager about why corners get cut at the start of a project. They stressed to me that time was a big factor, their staff were so busy with their day to day that they didn't have time to follow the correct procedures and processes that had been laid out by the business. Being sensitive to their overall frustrations I asked this manager what they thought of the business' processes. Their reply was that in an ideal world the processes would be great and that they would really help the business to improve its performance. I then asked how many of their rush tasks that were keeping their staff so busy were as a result of the processes not being followed at the outset (a little bit of cause and effect thinking) and the expression on the manager's face was priceless. Please note that I don't have these kinds of conversations for my own personal kicks, but when someone's facial expression changes because the 'penny has dropped' I do enjoy seeing the epiphany take place. The fact was that, like many people, they are stuck in a loop of cape wearing activity because they haven't spotted the relationship between what they haven't done and what they need to do in order to get off this particular merry-go-round.

If you find yourself in a similar situation with your business' processes being ignored due to your staff being 'too busy', then it might be time to draw some links between the current fire-fighting activities and the formalised process steps that haven't been undertaken. When the cause and effect relationship is identified, and acknowledged, it can help to change behaviours and hence results. This approach also helps facilitate the human resources angle of either supporting and coaching your staff to embrace and use your business' processes or to have the other conversation about whether there is a good fit between the business and the individual in question. Hopefully the links between your business processes and your results will be identified, their design being acknowledged as not having happened by accident, and (eventually) these processes being embraced.

Combining this realisation with the management of the processes in a robust and disciplined way (through your possible restructuring of who reports to whom) is a great strategy to help you experience a relatively cape-less working environment.

It doesn't stop, this is for life!

As I have referred to discipline and routine you may have figured out that living with fewer capes in your working life means that this approach is a style. This isn't a one-time fix never to be reviewed again, this is a way of life. I know this from my first-hand experience as a manager and as a witness of businesses that talk the talk, but don't walk the walk.

As already mentioned, the changes you make to improve the discipline, routine, measures and structure in your business to support this kind of working might not always work out brilliantly the first time around. This is normal and, realistically, it is to be expected. What it means is that you need to review what you have learned from the changes that you made, tweak your plan and then try again with your improvement. What it definitely doesn't mean is that you allow your teams to revert to the previous ways of working.

For example, a gentleman in one of my clients' businesses was a big fan of doing things himself. Self-sufficiency is often a desirable trait, but not when it limits the team's capacity. In this case, whenever a problem was identified in the quality of the work of this person's colleagues he would suck all of their work back in so that it could be done 'properly'. The fallacy of this was the person supposedly doing the work 'properly' was not always correct, but their personality influenced his colleagues to the point that they accepted that this was the way it was going to be. Over time this position would relax and the work would eventually creep back out to the surrounding team members. In the short-term it put huge pressure on this one person, under-utilised the surrounding staff and created a bottleneck through this part of the process.

This person is still a big fan of doing things himself, but

through the combination of measures (including workload by person), team meetings and a firm manager this situation is now managed. When problems arise, they are reviewed and any changes that need to be made are made and the capacity under-load / over-load situation is now avoided.

So, now that we have looked at some wider business issues, and how to monitor the health of your business, we'll now take a short look at you and your personality!

Action Points

- Review your Key Performance Indicators and ensure that you have an adequate coverage of process metrics.
- Ensure that you have an appropriate spread of routine business meetings organised, to keep your process management activities at cause.
- Review the structure of your business and identify any arrangements that don't help you to operate in a disciplined and orderly manner, and re-structure as required.

Are You Suffering from Low Intolerance?

During this book I have taken you on a journey through a range of strategies that you can deploy to improve how your business operates. I have looked at the cause and effect nature of business chaos, defining utopian visions to help pull your staff in the right direction and ways to both implement your plans and to keep your results where you want them.

However, please let me share with you a very specific behaviour that may have a strong impact on your business' results going forward. I am going to look at how you affect the working standards of the business.

Why do we put up with the status quo?

How is your status quo? I could imagine that if you have decided to read this book then you would like your normal days to be a little different. So, why do so many people put up with work the way it is?

There are many answers to this question.

Some people don't know any better. You can show them new ways of working and in many cases, you can get a different result by doing that.

Some people don't want to do any better. You can coach them, support them and, if they still don't change, part company with them. There are options for this issue too.

Some people have given up. With the right circumstances, leadership and support these people can get onboard with your changes.

Some people haven't realised that things have slipped. These are the people I want to speak to in this chapter.

We often don't notice degradation...

A few weeks ago, I re-arranged my garden and I chose to power wash my patio. I didn't think that the flagstones looked too bad, and in the spirit of trying to do a proper job with my household chores I thought I would invest an hour to give them a clean.

It turned out that they were filthy!

The contrast between the flagstones that I cleaned and those that I hadn't gotten to yet was staggering. They didn't look dirty until I cleaned one and saw what a clean one actually looked like. My wife noticed too and we got to enjoy our clean and fresh looking patio.

The point is that I didn't actually think that they were dirty in the first place and thought I would only get marginal results if I did clean them. I was seriously out of sync with reality!

What is there in your business that is like this too? Are there small things that you walk past every day, or participate in, that just aren't as good as they used to be? Do you go to meetings and nod your head instead of challenging the content of the meeting? Do you have a maintenance system that doesn't stop the machines from breaking down as well as it used to do? Do you have staff appraisals that have lost their zest and ability to get your team excited?

What is there that you need to re-invigorate?

Normal degrades over time

Most improvements suffer from this effect. The good intentions on day one can soon fade after a few days when the stresses and strains of business life kick in. You can see this clearly with new starters in a business. A new manager joins a business, full of enthusiasm and ideals, and months later they have become just the same as everyone else. Not only have they 'fitted in', but with additional workload now undertaken, a number of their original small (causal) tasks get dropped from their habits. The risk here is that these small items get missed off and that they have a big impact in terms of their results longer term…

Likewise, projects can fail before they become embedded. When the project reaches a conclusion the result it is producing (let's say that the project was to improve the delivery of a business service) is often at its best. If the team suffers from having poor habits and experience a few problems the revised service delivery may well become compromised over time.

Instructions can ebb away too. What people think that they remember and what the full instruction is can be two different things. I can think of countless examples where even just a day or two can be enough to dislodge clear instruction and logic from the minds of a busy person and lead them back into a state of confusion and error. One shining example of this was when I was helping a business sort out its Bills of Materials (the information a manufacturing computer system uses to manage its ordering and inventory). The lady who was responsible for inputting the information was making record progress and frankly I was stunned that she could have done it so fast. Beaming, she showed me how she carried out the work. I thought she was going to show me a shortcut that I wasn't aware of, but unfortunately, she wanted to show me just how fast she could input data (like how millennials can text at the speed of light!). What I noticed was that she was missing out 50% of the work. The early days of the input were correct. She had the Standard Operating Procedure right in front of her and yet her mind had truncated the process. Unfortunately for the business the work had to be re-done and the overall migration of this particular project had to be delayed as a result.

Whether the degradation is through ignorance, being stretched, a lack of education about the processes, or whatever, it is useful as a principle to bear in mind. If you are aware that what you call normal today might not have been acceptable in the past and most likely won't be acceptable at some point in the future, you will be well poised to keep this issue from derailing your business' processes. If your business is one of the few that can keep on improving day in day out without any real difficulty then keeping this up your sleeve anyway will just mean that you are even more prepared for your onward journey of improved performance levels.

Get upset about things

The title of this section is meant to sound a little backwards. When you realise that standards are dropping in your business I don't want you to be OK with this situation. I don't want you to have a high tolerance level for this kind of thing, I want you to have a low tolerance level so that you can trigger an appropriate response. This response should be one that can help steer your business back onto the right tracks and to a higher level of results. In many cases I would hope that this response would steer you into some of the topics and methods I have shared in this book.

The important factor in you personally making a difference is that, if you have let certain activities drop in your business, by becoming conscious of what has been dropped and what needs to be done about it, you can increase your effectiveness as a manager. A change in how you see the world around you, from a position of what is acceptable can make a big difference.

Once you have spotted standards that have slipped you need to be able to help set the right standards and encourage and cajole your team so that the standards can be achieved once more. Whilst I suggest that you embrace being unhappy with the situation so that you can re-focus your energies in the right directions please don't get hooked on always being critical / negative about what is going on around you. Be upset, but not difficult, annoying or destructive in the process.

Who has the most stringent standards?

The standards that you exude are by far one of the best ways to encourage change in your business. If you are telling everyone to behave in a certain way, but are spotted not living and breathing the same experience then your credibility will be shot and you will have a hard time encouraging others to behave as you want them to.

A few months ago I was talking to a Health and Safety Manager about some of the issues that they were dealing with, that had already triggered a number of cape-wearing situations. As the conversation carried on it turned out that this person was unable to organise some very important training because of production demands getting in the way. A comment was made that production came first, and this came out of the mouth of the Health and Safety Manager! Everyone else knew that safety came first and that production needed to be halted. Standards had dropped and this conversation made this abundantly clear. You'll be pleased to know that the training was organised immediately after this conversation.

If you are going to lead your business away from the unnecessary capes then it is essential that you have standards that are appropriate to your business. I used to say that you would need to have the highest standards, and whilst this phrase works for most businesses there have been occasions when standards have been taken to the nth degree and this can lead to inefficiencies occurring. I am sure that you will take a sensible stance on this, but please make sure that you live and breathe a way of working that at least meets the standards that your business needs to work properly.

If you need to push the punctuality of meetings starting on time, don't be late for them yourself.

If reporting cycles are being ignored, don't skip an update.

If some frank conversations need to be had in the business, don't shy away.

I'm sure that you get the picture.

Put your intolerance to good use... become evangelical

Look at all of the areas in your business that you have identified as having slipped and brainstorm ways that you can bring the standards back to where they need to be. Find ways, more specifically, to behave in a way that doesn't allow standards to slip in the first place. What do you need to work on in order to do this?

Becoming evangelical, as discussed a couple of chapters ago, is a great way to promote standards, once you have ironed out any bugs in your own approach. After you have identified all of the issues that you can see in the business that are related to dropped standards and have been (up to now) tolerated by yourself, list out what changes you need to make personally in order to be a shining example of what high standards looks like.

Leave reminders, formalise meeting agendas, develop your routines, link your KPIs, do whatever it takes to show everyone that you are the king or queen of high standards. High standards mean that the causal tasks the business needs to undertake are done in the right way by people that care about the results and have professional pride. Businesses need more people like this, so lead them by being the archetype of this behaviour.

We're nearing the end of our journey together, but before I conclude this book let me take you for a quick ride into the future.

Action Points

- Look generally at your business and ask yourself if there are any areas, or activities, where standards have dropped. Plan how you want to reverse this situation.
- Look at yourself and identify any standards that you have personally dropped and develop a plan to address this.
- Watch out for signs that others are lowering their standards and nip this behaviour in the bud.

What Does Good Look Like Now?

By now you should have a different view of how your business can operate and deliver its products and services. The key difference, and the intention of this book, is that you can deliver your products and services with fewer cape-wearing episodes. I like the phrase 'what does good look like?' and I want you to reflect on where you are now before I wrap this book up. Hopefully good means something different than what your normal business days looked like before you started this journey.

This chapter is a quick stop off to make sure that the changes you are about to make in your business are as effective as possible and double check that what looked good to you when you started reading this book still looks good now. This short chapter is a pause to let you look back at what you have created, if you have developed your ideas whilst you have been following this book, and allow you to refine your ideas before you launch them.

Go back to your compass

I want you to think about the vision(s) you created for your business, the utopian state that you defined for the business. Have the action plans that you defined provided a clear path to allow you to reach the utopian state that is desired? If you think that you need some additional actions, mini-projects, or task groups then please identify what needs to happen and get that planned and scheduled.

Assess your readiness

Are you ready to get rid of the capes? Are you ready to guide your teams to victory and implement the changes that you have planned? Are you ready to raise your standards and hold others accountable to keep their part of the bargain too?

Change takes effort, focus and persistence (as well as prioritisation, communication, creativity and any other positive activity that you can think of). I want you to make sure that you are ready. If you don't feel ready then, assuming this isn't a timing issue for you or the business, can you find some partners that can help you deliver the changes? Is there a colleague in a sister department that you can rely on for support, or a mentor higher up in the business who can be your sounding-board?

You can always start small and build up when it comes to change, but be honest with yourself before you dive into the changes and do your best to stack the odds in your favour.

Turn actions into habits

Do you know how you are going to turn the new / revised actions (causes) that will give you the results (effects) that you want into embedded habits? Have you got enough other habits and routines in your business currently that will allow you to piggy back the new activities and help convert them into habits?

As I have mentioned numerous times in this book already, beware of the natural feral state that your team members may exhibit when the going gets tough. You need to get to a point where not doing a task feels alien and doing the task is the new natural preference. Peer pressure can work well here to keep new working patterns on track and having a few allies / champions to help you implement the nitty gritty parts of the changes is essential.

With a handful of good people helping you to implement the hands-on part of your changes you can accomplish great things.

Linking your vision to your daily actions

Being able to convert your utopian view into reality means that there needs to be a clear link between the actions you undertake each day and the vision you are aiming for. When you review the routines and how you will undertake your improvement projects, will you and your team be able to make continual strides (or baby steps, if required) towards that vision? This kind of change can't be done occasionally, it needs to become part of what the working day is all about – it needs to become the working day.

The habits that you will help to shape will become the utopian future's causes, so that you can realise the utopian future's effects. The projects that you have identified are there to either lift up your performance in a specific area and / or to nudge a habit in the right direction. When you boil down process management you can summarise it as two things:
-   Routines to keep the process being managed correctly.
-   Projects to boost performance and / or correct the routines.

So, have you got sufficient links between your vision and your daily habits, going forward, so that you can make the transition (from a process management perspective)?

Refine your guiding principles

Near the start of our journey together I asked you to compile a list of guiding principles. These were the 'productive truths' that could help steer your business away from the need to wear capes and into a more efficient and more effective state.

Now that you have reached the end of this book I would like you to review your list and see if any changes need to be made to the collection of principles that you have brought together. Having an effective list is a really powerful tool when you have team meetings and issues arise that need decisions to be made. Having a good set of guiding principles allows you to re-direct your teams swiftly and can make for very focused and very efficient improvement activity.

Is there anything you want to change, or add, to your list of principles? Remember, that having just a handful of appropriate principles can be all you need to revolutionise how your business performs.

Scheduling your next review

Time moves on and so do businesses. What seems like a good idea today will not be a guaranteed perfect fit in several months', or years', time. As with the title of this section, 'what does good look like now?' is the question that I want you to ask yourself again and again over the upcoming years.

I doubt that your business will be exactly the same this time next year (or even in six months from now) and the questions asked specifically in this section are worth asking again. Your vision may be refined further, there might be new products and services launched that require different (or additional) routines to be forged. You might need to be on your third revision of your guiding principles, once your teams have embraced them and started to contribute to the shaping of those principles. Better habits might be identified and bad ones may have appeared.

Scheduling your reviews now is a relatively straightforward ask. Scheduling your reviews nearer the time will most likely be a challenge. So, I encourage you to have a look at your calendar now and decide what would make sense to you.

Launching a course of improvement is always the challenge, until you build enough momentum to carry you forward to your utopia. With this in mind I would recommend that you have your initial reviews close together and then eventually space them out, something like the following:
- Weekly for the first month.
- Fortnightly for months two and three.
- Monthly for months four, five and six.
- Quarterly for the next half of a year (reviews in months 9 and 12).
- Six monthly thereafter.

Get ready to go!

As with all of the commentary in this book, do what works for your business. The experience I have had with this kind of approach is that you will need to put in a lot of extra effort to steer your teams away from what they are doing today and towards what they should be doing to re-align your days with your vision.

I'm sure also that as you have been reading this book you have realised some priorities that you could focus on within your business, to both make your life easier and to reduce the future cape-wearing instances. You might even want to undertake these actions before you work your way more formally through the ideas in this book. These immediate priorities might include:
- Getting some allies around you.
- Identifying the easy to complete, quick results generating, projects that will get some traction right from the start.
- Developing some simple strategies to help you protect some time to deliver your projects.
- Dealing with your tricky staff, ensuring that they want to come along on this journey.

Ok, I think you're just about set. Before I share my closing thoughts, let me recap on the key principles in this book, so that you have a quick reference guide to fall back on when you feel like you have veered off the beaten track.

Action Points

- Check that you are happy with the vision that you have created.
- Double check that you know what you are in for, with whom, when you start your journey to improve how your processes are managed going forward.

- Make sure that you know how you are going to link your actions to your vision and that they are included into your newly revised routines.
- Prime your guiding principles, ready for use.
- Schedule your reviews.
- Use this section as a checklist periodically through your implementation activities in order to keep on track.

Pulling This All Together

Before I give you my final thoughts on the challenges of eliminating the unnecessary capes from our business lives, let me share with you a summary of the principles contained in this book.

The intention of this summary of the key points of the book is to give you an easy to use reference as you go through your journey. It isn't a summary of each chapter, just the main points / principles that will make a difference to your business.

Cape spotting

Being aware that cape wearing exists in your business is often enough to get the ball rolling. Whenever there is an issue in your business that requires a super-hero performance to resolve it, determine whether it is an unnecessary cape, or not. If it is unnecessary, use it as a trigger to follow through the remaining points, or add it to your list of things to improve for later.

Living at cause

This is the essential consideration we must all review. Do you want to operate primarily at cause, conducting your activities in a way that is controllable and manageable? Reacting to events indicates that this balance is out of kilter and should direct your focus to where you need to improve.

Having a vision

Giving your business a view of your utopian vision, to head towards, does two main things in the context of reducing the number of cape wearing episodes being faced. The first thing (and the primary reason) is to guide people to where you need them to go to once they get past the immediate troubles being experienced. The second thing is to help paint a picture for those team members worried / confused / scared about where you want to take the business to. Some people won't find it easy to get past okay and this element of the change process is about helping people see what moving from Okay to great looks like.

Guiding principles

When ideas to improve are becoming scarce, disagreements are forming and frustrations are building, the guiding principles you have devised are there to steer people back to the essence of how the business needs to operate. A good set of guiding principles should be communicated, debated and used to focus your activities as your business requires.

Proper projects

Prioritising your improvement opportunities, to reduce the number of capes your business has to experience on a daily, or weekly, basis is essential. The improvement projects should be in line with your guiding principles and be designed to help move your business from where it is now towards your utopian state. Even the simplest of tweaks to your improvement plans, to include deadlines and accountability, will make a huge difference to your results if you can see the improvements through. I know that you want this, so don't let me (or yourself) down!

Developing better habits and routines

Different results require different ways of working, and forming good habits through defining your routines is one way to achieve this. It is an approach that I recommend; in my experience businesses that have great results have formalised routines being executed every day. Businesses that don't have great results (but plenty of cape wearing superheroes) often haven't formally considered the routines that are in their business. Processes need routines in order for them to be triggered and operated. Processes that are effective and operating at 'cause' definitely do.

Building the reporting system

Asking how things are going shouldn't be one of your questions in the medium term. You should know how things are going already because of the reporting approach that you have tied into your routines. Process driven KPIs, that include the process itself and its inputs, should be helping you to make real-time decisions that can help you achieve a better outcome. Reporting shouldn't be heavy, but it should certainly help you more than it hinders you and should definitely be designed to give you a massive return on your efforts by making correct decisions that avert the need to wear a cape.

Keeping the conversations alive

Change is difficult for most of us and having a dialogue with your team as they progress through their journey is important to the success of the changes you want to make. Formal project reviews can be interspersed with informal catch ups and group debates about how things are going. If your team are confused, scared, excited, fearful, stuck, de-motivated, proud, or whatever, let these discussions take place. Learn from them and help your team through the process of change. Don't let misunderstanding and confusion kill the momentum of the changes taking place, otherwise you run the risk of your team 'going feral' and embracing the capes they remember so well.

Leading from the front

Leadership is a simple concept if you consider it as being 'knowing where you are going' and 'going first'. Tie this perspective in with being evangelical about the changes that need to take place. You don't have to be in everyone's face and making a nuisance of yourself as you do this, but you can be pro-active and enthused about making the changes work. The alternative of being negative, or indifferent, will not help you make the changes you need to make, so please choose to embrace your leadership role in this mission.

Dip-checks for 'looking good' and pulling yourself back on track

Keep an eye out for where you are going to on your improvement journey. Keep looking for signs of success and share these with your team. If someone is doing a great job tell them and then allow them to make even more of a positive impact on your improvement opportunities. If someone is off track then help them to get back on track. The improvement activity doesn't just live in the review meetings that you are running, the improvements should be felt each and every day as you work to improve the fabric of the day itself.

Raising the standards

Stop putting up with unacceptable behaviours and practices and swallow them up as part of your cape-freeing adventure. Have standards that are higher than what you need (without stifling the business) and help others to live up to these standards. Make sure that you are an exemplar in this regard and let the standards, along with your guiding principles, take you to your utopian experience.

Committing to never stopping

And, finally, don't let yourself get to a point where you think you are done. If you feel this way, find a successor and let them take the lead. Plan in regular reviews (at a frequency that supports your point in your journey) and keep on checking to see if you have reached utopia, or another place that looks good. Life and business keeps on moving and changing and there is no real end to the improvement process. Stick with it; in the short-term you will get some pain, in the medium-term you will get some great results and in the long-term you will become a true hero (but one that doesn't need a cape).

Have you got all of that? Come back to this section as often as you need, and keep yourself on the straight and narrow.

Ok, it's time for my final thoughts…

Final Thoughts

Here we are, at the end of the book. I hope that you have found the ideas to be useful and you can see yourself using them to help you transform how your business works. I have been in a few crunch positions in the past, and I do not believe that relying purely on a 'the cape is the way' attitude is one that can bring about long-lasting results. I believe that thinking our way out of problems and acting at cause in a cool and controlled manner is far more efficient and effective in the long run.

So, here are my final words on this subject (in this book at least!).

The cape will always exist

It will. I have to live with this fact and so do you. But, the difference is in whether it is an essential cape (that we couldn't have foreseen / planned for) or an unnecessary cape (that is the result of us getting in our own way). Don't freak out at the occasional cape (the world hasn't broken!) and don't go back to what you were doing before (unless you have had a mad moment and created a ludicrous plan).

We can all live with the need to wear the essential capes that come along, be fit enough to leap into action when you absolutely must leap into action. Choose not to live with the capes that we have to wear as a result of our own poor judgement, cutting corners and being undisciplined.

Expect fewer capes, not none.

There is a way forward

This book shares with you a route you can follow to move away from chaos and regular cape wearing. There are other routes too. The key to remember here is that if you are feeling overwhelmed and under pressure from re-active problems that your business faces then there will be a way out of this situation.

Embrace the ideas in this book and use the previous chapter frequently to keep yourself on the right track. Pick and mix the ideas and strategies I have shared with you throughout this book and create your own approach.

There is a way forward and the destination is worth the journey.

There will be some that don't want to join you

This is a fact of life. Don't worry about it as they will fall into two main camps.

Some will not want to join you initially. As more of your team get onboard and they start to see results these initial antagonists will change their mind and defect to the side of the good guys (that's you, if you hadn't realised!).

Some will never want to join you. If they don't get in the way and don't detract from your mission to improve your business you may choose to live with them. If they do detract then you can determine whether they aren't following 'reasonable management requests' and see where the conversation takes you.

It won't be personal if people don't want to join you. Some are scared, some are lazy, some are confused and some will have views that oppose yours. Do your best to have plans that make sense, are achievable and have an implementation that fits in with your normal day to day working.

There will be a lot that will want to join you

On the other hand, you will most likely find that there are a great deal of people who are ready for a change. They will want to work in a more professional and productive environment. An environment where it doesn't take blood, sweat and tears to achieve mediocre results. They will be waiting for someone to come along and show them a path to a better way of working.

The leader is you and the time to do this is now. Use the methods in this book to help illuminate this path and allow your colleagues to get onboard with the journey. Some of them will want to help lead and others will be happy participating. Find a role for each of these individuals and reduce the time it will take to complete the first stage of your journey (before you get into ongoing reviews and continuous improvement, that is).

Enjoy the process

The journey may take some time. It might also deviate wildly from your original plans and take you off course. This is why I have asked you to create a set of guiding principles and a view of utopia. These two tools work as a compass so that you can always create a new plan and get back on track. Accept that this is a highly likely part of the journey, relax and try to enjoy the process as much as you can.

During your journey there is a good chance that you will learn some new things. You will most likely learn something about yourself during the process of the changes. You will very likely learn how your colleagues respond to challenges and the pressure of balancing experimentation in your business and keeping on top of the day job. You will learn what works and what doesn't work for your business. You can get lots of things out of the journey, things that can help you become a better and more effective individual going forward.

If you keep going with your changes you will reach a point where you can say that you have won, so enjoy the process of change and all the rewards it can bring with it. If you can convert these new skills into a promotion, recognition, better profits, happier customers, an easier life or a whole new career then that would be icing on the cake, wouldn't it?

Farewell, for now

This is where I am going to leave you now.

The journey ahead is yours to take without me.

If you think my views and strategies have merit then I will feel like I have done my job. Thank you for reading this book and I wish you all the best for your improvement adventure.

I would really like to find out how you have got on with using these approaches, so if you feel like getting in touch to tell me how you got on please do so. You can email me directly at **gilesjohnston@smartspeed.co.uk**.

I'd like to think that the business cape wearing status quo is on its way out. Let's see if we can make this a reality!

All the best,

Giles

Links

The following links may be useful to you as you make progress with your improvements:

Systems and Processes

To find other resources, information on my other books, toolkits and courses visit:
http://www.systemsandprocesses.co.uk/

Free OTIF report

Sign up for my regular email newsletter and get your copy of my free guide "You're Late!!!'. It includes seven low cost / quick to implement strategies to help your business improve both its productivity and its delivery performance. Follow this link to get your copy:
http://www.systemsandprocesses.co.uk/free-on-time-delivery-improvement-guide/

Blog

News, ideas and improvement methods are all shared on my blog. You can read it at:
http://www.systemsandprocesses.co.uk/blog/

Twitter

For those of you who embrace social media, you can get my tweets by following me using the handle @betterfasternow. https://twitter.com/betterfasternow

Giles Johnston

Giles is a Chartered Engineer with a background in Production Engineering and Operations Management. He spends most of his time working on Lean, ERP and Operations Management improvement projects.

Giles has worked in a variety of different roles within manufacturing prior to working as a consultant for a prestigious university.

In 2005 Giles decided to forge his own path and created Smartspeed, which has been helping businesses to improve their delivery performance and productivity levels, along with their profits, ever since.

Giles can be contacted by:
Email -   **gilesjohnston@smartspeed.co.uk**
Website -   **www.smartspeed.co.uk**

Recommended Reading

To supplement this book, I recommend that you consider reading the following books:

Covey, S. (2004) *The 7 Habits of Highly Effective People*. Simon and Schuster.

Bicheno, J et al (2016) *The Lean Toolbox*. 5th Edition. Picsie Books.

Johnston, G (2013) *Sunrise Meetings*. Amazon Media.

Koch, R (2002) *The 80/20 Principle*. Image Books.

Womack, P and Jones, D (2003) *Lean Thinking*. New Ed. Simon and Schuster.

Johnston, G (2012) *Business Process Re-engineering*. Amazon Media

Index

www.ingramcontent.com/pod-product-compliance
Lightning Source LLC
Chambersburg PA
CBHW020906180526
45163CB00007B/2640